START TRADING
OPTIONS

START TRADING OPTIONS

A Self-Teaching Guide for Trading Options Profitably

Kevin M. Kraus

McGraw-Hill
New York • Chicago • San Francisco • Lisbon • London • Madrid •
Mexico City • Milan • New Delhi • San Juan • Seoul • Singapore •
Sydney • Toronto

The **McGraw-Hill** Companies

Copyright © 2006 by The McGraw-Hill Companies, Inc. All rights reserved. Printed in the United States of America. Except as permitted under the United States Copyright Act of 1976, no part of this publication may be reproduced or distributed in any form or by any means, or stored in a database or retrieval system, without the prior written permission of the publisher.

3 4 5 6 7 8 9 0   DOC/DOC   0 9 8

ISBN 0-07-145909-X

McGraw-Hill books are available at special quantity discounts to use as premiums and sales promotions, or for use in corporate training programs. For more information, please write to the Director of Special Sales, Professional Publishing, McGraw-Hill, Two Penn Plaza, New York, NY 10121-2298. Or contact your local bookstore.

Library of Congress Cataloging-in-Publication Data
Kraus, Kevin M.
  How to start trading options : a self-teaching guide for trading options
profitably / by Kevin M. Kraus.
     p. cm.
  ISBN 0-07-145909-X (pbk. : alk. paper)
  1. Stock options. I. Title.
  HG6042.K728 2005

332.64'53—dc22   2005004734

For Gayle Marie
—for all your love and support

"An investment in knowledge always pays the best interest"
– Benjamin Franklin

CONTENTS

CHAPTER **1** Market Basics   1

What Are Commodities?   1

Derivative Contracts   2

Who's Who in Futures   3

The Exchanges   4

The Trading   5

Commodity Pricing   7

Key Terms   9

Chapter Test   10

Answers to Tests   12

CHAPTER **2** Option Basics   15

What Are Options?   15

Calls and Puts   18

Market Quotes and Option Premium   19

"The Money"   21

Option Value—Intrinsic versus Time   23

Time Value and Time Decay   25

Implied Volatility   26

Option Delta   29

Key Terms   32

Chapter Test   33

Answers to Tests   34

CHAPTER **3** Buying and Selling Options   37

Buying Options   37

Buying Calls   39

Buying Puts   42

Breakeven on Purchased Options   46

Liquidating Options   51

Using Proper Order Terminology   52

Selling Options   53

Selling Call Options   56

Selling Put Options   59

Calculating Breakeven for Short Options   60

Offsetting Prior to Expiration   62

Offsetting to Control Risk   63

Key Terms   64

Chapter Test   65

Answers to Tests   67

CHAPTER **4** Option Spreads Strategies   69

Vertical Spreads   69

Risk Reversal Spreads   76

Aggressive Delta   78

Sell, Buy, Sell Vertical Spreads   82

Ratio Call Spreads   85

The Delta Effect   91

Multiple Option Ratio Spreads   92

Butterfly Spreads   93

Back Spreads   97

Long Strangles   100

Short Strangles   104

Long Straddles   106

Short Straddles   109

Credit Spreads   111

Condor Spreads   114

Key Spread Strategies and Terms   116

Chapter Test   116

Answers to Tests   118

CHAPTER **5** Advanced Strategies 123
  Multiple Option Strategy 123
  Calendar Spreads 129
  Volatility Analysis—Market Weight 131
  Option Forecasting 135
  Forecasting with Time Value Decay 137
  Combinations of Futures and Options 139
  Covered Options 143
  Futures Covered Risk Reversal 144
  Synthetic Futures 146
  Chapter Test 146
  Answers to Tests 148

CHAPTER **6** Risk Management 151
  Time Value Management 151
  Risk-Management Strategies 153
  Stop Orders 153
  Market Price Monitoring 154
  Premium Levels 155
  Monitoring Risk Points 155
  Taking Profits 156
  Hedging Basics 157
  Option Hedging Techniques 158
  Option Trading Tips 164
  Final Exam 166
  Answers to Exam 171

Index 173

CHAPTER 1

MARKET BASICS

In this chapter we begin with some basic market information and concepts. We define commodities and derivative contracts and explain supply and demand, market fundamentals, the exchanges, and futures trading. Your option education begins with the basics of derivative contracts and market economics. In Chapter 1 we will cover:

- What are commodities
- Derivative contracts
- Supply and demand
- Market fundamentals
- The commodity exchanges
- Futures trading

WHAT ARE COMMODITIES?

Before beginning your option education we want to cover the basics of derivative contracts and basic market economics. First let's cover what commodities are and how they relate to the futures industry. Commodities are very simply things that are consumed or processed in the manufacture or production of products.

For example: ABC Steel company uses iron ore in the production of steel. Iron is a commodity, although it is not commonly traded on futures exchanges. A bakery company uses wheat from a grain miller in the production of bread. Wheat is a commodity commonly traded on futures exchanges. Most everything you

FIGURE 1-1

look at or use is a commodity, many of them traded on commodity exchanges somewhere in the world. Everything from the gold in your ring to the milk in your refrigerator is a commodity.

Commodities are typically described as agricultural or mining products; however, in today's market the term *commodity* has come to describe many agricultural, food, energy, mining, and financial products.

DERIVATIVE CONTRACTS

When people talk about trading commodities they are referring to trading derivative contracts, more commonly known as futures. *Derivatives*, or *futures*, are contract instruments between two parties for the exchange of a commodity whether it be a physical commodity like wheat or a financial instrument like a 10-year Treasury note or a foreign currency. The instrument must specify certain things in order to qualify as a futures contract:

- Commodity
- Quantity
- Quality

- Time of delivery
- Point of delivery

Futures contracts do not specify the price. The price of the contract is determined in open market trade on a futures exchange. Here is an example of a current futures contract:

Chicago Board of Trade December #2 Yellow Corn 5000bu contract. (Symbol CZ5)

- Commodity = Yellow Corn
- Quantity = 5000 bushels
- Quality = #2
- Time of delivery = 3d Friday in December 2005
- Point of delivery = CBOT designated site

If you enter a contract to purchase 10 new pink yard flamingos in your neighbor's garage next Thursday, essentially you are entering a futures contract. If another neighbor offered to purchase the contract to buy the flamingos from you, at a higher price, then you would keep the difference and would have traded your contract. Remember, the essential elements are commodity, quantity, quality, time of delivery, point of delivery.

There are two types of futures contracts, those that provide for physical delivery of a particular commodity and those that call for an eventual cash settlement rather than delivery. Many futures contracts have gone to cash settlement recently as the scope of the market has increased beyond a local producer level. Cash settlement futures maintain the terms we listed above, only the delivery point is replaced by cash settlement. In reality, today's traders do not often involve themselves in delivery situations on delivery-type contracts as many speculators do not want to take or make delivery. Rather, the vast majority of traders choose to realize their gains or losses by buying or selling an offsetting futures contract prior to the delivery date.

WHO'S WHO IN FUTURES

In the early days of future trading, the contracts involved mostly producers and end users of commodity products who resolved prices through open market bid and offer in an open auction. These people, known as *hedgers*, have a vested interest in a commodity product as a producer, end user, or middle business. In today's market, active futures trade still continues among hedgers in many forms. Some are small- and medium-size operations. In agriculture this would be small farmers, ranchers, or co-ops. In the financial sector, it might be an independent mortgage company or a corporation trading goods overseas and exchanging currencies. Today there are also large-scale hedgers such as regional, national, or international corporations with vested interests in commodity markets as they are somewhere in the supply or demand chain. We refer to these hedgers as *commercials*.

In modern markets we also have traders in futures contracts called *speculators*. Speculators are those with strictly monetary interests in the activity of the market without having any vested interest in the commodity being traded. Speculators vary in size and trading capability as well. There are individual speculators trading small quantities, but there are also groups of speculators, investment firms and wealthy individuals with large capital, often called *funds*. Funds and commercials tend to supply the market with large-scale liquidity and can have a dramatic effect on market activity, although many times these two powerhouse groups are on opposite sides of the market.

THE EXCHANGES

Commodity futures contracts are traded at commodity exchanges in various places around the country. *Exchanges* are organized marketplaces for trading

---

TEST YOUR KNOWLEDGE 1-1
(Answers are at end of each chapter.)

1. Crude oil is an example of a commodity. True or False?
2. Futures contracts specify commodity, quantity, quality, price. True or False?
3. Speculators have a vested interest in the commodity being traded. True or False?
4. A large corporate grain hedger might be considered a _____.
5. Locals or floor traders create _____ in the market.

commodities. Historically, they were sites for cash commodity trades as well, although this has been reduced to very minimal trade in recent years. The largest exchanges are in Chicago and New York

The majority of United States contracts are traded on four exchanges, the Chicago Board of Trade (CBOT), Chicago Mercantile Exchange (CME), New York Mercantile Exchange (NYMEX), and New York Board of Trade (NYBOT). There are two regional exchanges the Kansas City Board of Trade (KCBOT) and the Minneapolis Grain Exchange (MGE) both focus mainly on regional wheat and feed commodities. The role of the exchange is to provide the standards for commodity futures such as quality, quantity, and delivery points. In addition, the exchange provides facilities known as a *trading floor* for futures and options to be traded.

Derivatives are traded in areas on the trading floor called *pits.* Here traders and brokers bid and offer for futures contracts in what is called *open outcry.* This is fairly literal, because the traders are using hand signals and shouting orders across the pit. This process of bid and offer is what establishes the price for futures. Each trade completed is posted and transmitted to quote systems around the world in seconds.

Today's exchange business is also done more and more by computer servers off the trading floor. Electronic-based markets continue to grow and are changing the way futures trade. Products like the Chicago Mercantile Exchange's' E-Mini S&P 500 pioneered electronic trading and are setting the standard for the markets of the future by providing fully automated trade execution and instantaneous trade reporting.

For each futures market, the commodity exchange sets the trading standards for margin requirements, trading hours, and trading regulations for each contract.

THE TRADING

On the floor, each pit usually has an area designated for each derivative or group of derivative contracts where the auction style or open outcry trading occurs. Contract months are often broken into different areas so more active contracts or contracts closer to expiration have an exclusive area and are typically larger to hold more traders. Traders refer to the closest contract to expiration as the front month. Contract representatives from clearing firms and trading companies around the world stand shoulder to shoulder bidding and offering for futures contracts and options.

In the pit, there are also independent traders often times referred to as *locals*. These traders work the floor for a living buying and selling futures and options in large volume for monetary gain. Locals are traditionally short-term players, many times out of the market each day or in and out of several positions during a single day. Locals are a valuable asset to traditional open outcry markets because they provide liquidity for traders off the floor. In the electronic markets, locals do not exist in a physical form. Liquidity is provided by electronic day traders speculating on the small moves of the market. The pure speed and accuracy of electronic trading creates an environment for small traders around the country to participate en masse like the locals in other markets. The trades are matched up by high-speed computers at the exchange.

When you place your order with your broker or trading system your order follows a fast-acting chain of events to get to the floor for trading.

- Your broker calls or transmits your order to a clerk on the side of the trading pit. Your order is than flashed by hand signal to a broker or assistant in the pit who offers it to the market.

- If your order gets filled, it is marked and reported to the clerk and returned back to your broker.

- In modernized markets, electronic orders go directly to the broker on the floor using an electronic handheld device which organizes the order for the broker to execute. If filled, the order is then returned via electronic transmission to the point of origin.

- Most brokers today have access to electronic trading systems or exclusively use electronic systems because of their speed and accuracy. Individual traders also have the opportunity with most brokerage firms to independently use electronic market access systems.

Another important function of exchanges is to provide services to the firms that represent individual or organization accounts. These companies called *clearing firms,* or more correctly *futures commission merchants,* are provided with reporting and settlements for contracts traded for the day in order to settle their individual accounts for the day's business. Clearing firms provide the accounting for each individual account, while the exchange assists in settling up the clearing firm's entire business for the session.

TEST YOUR KNOWLEDGE 1-2

1. An exchange sets the standard for futures contracts. True or False?
2. Locals trade independently on the floor buying and selling for individual gain. True or False?
3. There are now only four commodity futures exchanges. True or False?
4. The area on the floor designated for each commodity is referred to as a _____?
5. A _____ _____ _____ provides individual daily accounting.

COMMODITY PRICING

The guiding factor for commodity pricing is the basic economics of supply and demand. The influence of supply and demand is felt in every aspect of a free market economy from commodity pricing to employment. We won't go through a complicated economic discussion of supply and demand, but we want to cover its relationship to general commodity pricing. Supply and demand is generally referred to as a fundamental market influence. A recent TV commercial for software nicely shows the influence of supply on market pricing. A winery manager is counting his aging bottles when a forklift accidentally knocks over rack after rack of wine bottles. The manager clicks a mouse and doubles the price of his wine at the distributor. The reduced future supply of wine means less wine to meet demand and higher prices.

When relating this to commodity futures, we designate supply and demand influences as fundamentals. These influences in the market are a driving factor to commodity futures pricing. Let's take a look at a very basic supply and demand concept in Figure 1-2.

The top section of Figure 1-2 shows that as supply rises, price tends to fall and as supply falls, price tends to rise. The influence of demand on price is a function of supply. As demand for a product rises, supplies tend to fall, forcing prices higher. Conversely, as demand decreases, product supplies rise and price tends to go down. This relationship is often why product and market

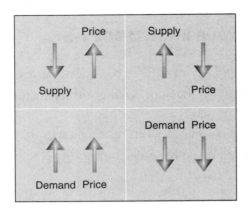

FIGURE 1-2
Supply and demand

prices cycle. As supply rises, price falls which often increases demand which once again reduces supply and increases price.

Consider supply and demand as the foundation of the market. In looking at grain pricing we see an example of the significant influence of supply and demand. If storage supplies of yellow corn are high, then grain elevators who store and market grain purchased from farmers, are likely to offer farmers or producers less for new grain supplies. If supplies are low, elevators may pay a premium to producers to make certain they can meet their own demand. At the exchange, traders will look at these factors and consider future supply and demand when bidding on contracts in the same way a grain elevator would.

This example of supply and demand translates across the board from agricultural and livestock products to monetary markets. Remember futures contracts are anticipating commodity pricing at some point in the future whether it be a month or years away. This anticipation is founded on analysis of future supply and demand for the underlying commodity. Also remember that these influences change day by day with changes in conditions, such as weather patterns, animal or crop problems, export changes, and mining discoveries.

There are a multitude of price influences in futures markets: expanded fundamental analysis of long-term trends in commodity production, political events, disease, social, environmental and health trends, etc. In recent years, political events have had more and more influence on U.S. economic conditions and demand for U.S. products. This continuously changes the supply and demand balance for importing and exporting agricultural and industrial products. Energy markets are an excellent example of how supply and demand as well as political influences create a highly volatile market. OPEC, terrorism, cold weather, drive season, freight prices, all push and pull the market price on a daily and intraday basis.

Another major market influence is the technical aspect of the market. Technical influences would relate to market patterns and cycles, volume, open interest, market trends, and dozens of technical analysis tools developed from mathematical and statistical sources which might position money at various pricing points on the market. These indications can be monetarily powerful in creating market momentum or in stopping market momentum. Many times it is difficult to draw barriers between technical and fundamental influences. Technical influences can often appear to be in the driver's seat of the market, at least in the short term. Remember long-term fundamentals have a long-term effect on the market, where technical influences may be more in the here and now. We recommend that you seek out additional educational material on technical trading and analysis to make sure you have a complete futures market education.

KEY TERMS

Commercial Large capital organization; corporate or private hedger

Commodity Products or materials that can be consumed, processed, or resold.

TEST YOUR KNOWLEDGE 1-3

1. In basic supply and demand, if supply falls price tends to fall. True or False?

2. An example of fundamental market influences would be market chart cycles. True or False?

3. Fundamentals are often long-term market indicators. True or False?

4. Chart patterns, indicators, and cycles are _____ indicators.

5. OPEC's raising crude oil production limits would likely _____ supply and _____ prices.

Derivative Contract instrument between parties for exchange of a commodity, derives value from the underlying commodity.

Exchange An organized marketplace for trading futures and options contracts or cash commodity products. Provides services for clearing merchant members.

Fund Large capital organization; corporate or wealthy speculator.

Fundamental Market influence based on changes in supply and demand or issues that could affect supply and demand such as weather changes, labor strikes, disease, health, and government spending.

Futures commission merchant (FCM) Provides clearing services for brokerage firms and trade execution services for individual and corporate hedgers and speculators.

Futures Common name for commodity, financial, currency, and index derivative contract products.

Hedger Party with a vested interest in the underlying commodity or instrument represented by the derivative, i.e., grain miller, mortgage bank.

Local Independent speculator working the trading floor.

Pit Section of trading floor for individual contracts or groups of contracts.

Speculator Party with only a monetary interest in the underlying commodity traded.

Technical Market influence based on analysis of cycles, statistics, and patterns on commodity-pricing charts.

Trading Floor Exchange-provided facility for execution of contract trade.

CHAPTER TEST

1. Which of the following are commodities?

   (a) Gold

   (b) Wheat

   (c) Instant pudding mix

   (d) All of the above

2. Which of the following is NOT a specification of a commodity futures contract?

   (a) Quality

   (b) Quantity

   (c) Price

   (d) Delivery terms

3. What is missing from the following futures contract specifications: ABC Commodity Exchange July #1 Blue Wheat Futures?

   (a) Quality

   (b) Quantity

   (c) Commodity

   (d) Delivery date

4. Who of the following has a vested interest in the markets?

   (a) Commercials

   (b) Locals

   (c) Funds

   (d) Speculators

5. Which of the following is not a current U.S. commodity exchange?

   (a) CBXE

   (b) CME

   (c) CBOT

   (d) NYMEX

6. Futures exchanges provide the following except?

   (a) Floor services

   (b) Contract specifications

(c) Individual accounting

(d) All of the above

7. Which of the following describes locals?

(a) Individual traders or firms who trade for monetary gain

(b) Active day traders on the floor of the exchange.

(c) Electronic traders on Internet-based systems

(d) a and b only

8. If supply of a particular commodity rises assuming demand hasn't changed you would normally expect prices to

(a) Do nothing

(b) Rise

(c) Fall

9. If the International Heart Organization announces that corn oil cures heart disease, you might expect corn prices to?

(a) Stay the same

(b) Rise

(c) Fall

(d) No way to know

10. Supply and demand is considered a?

(a) Technical influence

(b) Fundamental influence

(c) Natural influence

ANSWERS TO TESTS

Test Your Knowledge 1-1

1. True. Crude oil is used in the production of energy products as well as plastics and chemicals. 2. False. Futures contracts denote commodity, quantity, quality, delivery time, and point of delivery, but not price. 3. False. Speculators have a monetary interest in a commodity being traded, but not a vested interest as a producer or end user (hedger) would. 4. Commercial. 5. Liquidity

Test Your Knowledge 1-2

1. True. Exchanges set the terms for each independent contract under the supervision of the Commodity Futures Trading Commission. 2. True. Locals are independent traders for personal gain. 3. False. There are several commodity futures exchanges, but there are four major exchanges in the United States.

Test Your Knowledge 1-3

1. False. When supplies fall, prices tend to rise. 2. False. Market chart cycles would be considered a technical influence. 3. True. Fundamentals can be short term, but overall their influence is long term even if the price effect is immediate. 4. Technical. 5. Raise supply, lower prices.

Chapter Test

1. d. Although the instant pudding is not traded as a futures contract, it is still a commodity under the definition of a commodity.
2. c. Price is determined by bid and offer or trade of a commodity, not by set specifications.
3. b. The quantity of the commodity is missing.
4. a. Commercials are large or corporate hedgers.
5. a. CBXE currently doesn't exist although it's similar to the stock market option exchange called the CBOE.
6. c. Individual accounting is provided by a futures commission merchant.
7. d. A and b apply. Electronic traders may simulate the role of locals in electronic markets but are not in the same category of trader.
8. c. When supply increases with static demand, prices tend to fall.
9. b. Rise. Corn oil demand would likely spike.
10. b. Fundamentals are things like supply and demand, weather, political, and market strength.

CHAPTER 2

OPTION BASICS

Let's continue with the basics about options. This introduction to options covers:

- What are options
- Understanding market quotes and option premium
- "The money"
- Option value
- Time decay
- Implied volatility
- Option delta

WHAT ARE OPTIONS?

Now that we have a little background on the futures market, we can look at the very basics of options and option trading. First let's look at the definition of an option:

> An option is a right, but not an obligation, to the underlying futures contract at a specified price and specified point in time.

Now let's take apart this definition. "An option is a right, but not an obligation." This statement applies to purchase options only. In our section about buying and selling options we'll cover short, or sold, options further. When you purchase an option, you are buying a right to the underlying futures contract. You are not obligated to the assignment of the futures contract. As the purchaser you have the right to exercise a purchased option into the underlying futures at any time or allow the option to expire without exercising.

"To the underlying futures contract" this part is simple; options are on the underlying futures contract, typically in the same contract month as the futures. For example: The December corn 220 call's underlying futures contract is the December CBOT corn futures. There are options called *serial options* which do not have an underlying contract month and revert to the next futures contract available. Serial options tend to have lower volume and open positions, or open interest, but are active in many futures contracts. An example would be, the January Japanese Yen 800 call that uses the underlying March Japanese yen contract because the futures are traded in March, June, September, and December only.

"At a specified price" this is the stated price at which an option can be exercised into a futures contract. This price is called the *strike price*. Figure 2-1 is a list of March CBOT corn calls. The strike price is listed in the Contract column. The *C* indicates that it is a call option and it shows the strike price. If you were to purchase a March corn 220 call option, you would have the right, but not the obligation, to purchase the March corn futures at 220.

Contract	Open	High	Low	Bid	Ask	Last
C-H05,C150						20092
C-H05,C160						2
C-H05,C170						1
C-H05,C180		247	247			247
C-H05,C190	136	157	136		136	157
C-H05,C200	80	85	70		72	85
C-H05,C205	26	26	26			26
C-H05,C210	40	43	34	40	35	43
C-H05,C215				15		
C-H05,C220	20	21	15	17	16	21
C-H05,C230	10	11	7	10	10	10
C-H05,C240	10	4	3	4		4
C-H05,C250	4	4	2	2	3	2

FIGURE 2-1
March corn calls

"At a specific point in time"—the specific point in time refers to the expiration date of the option contract. Exercise of an option into the underlying futures contract must occur on or before the expiration date, otherwise the option is considered expired. Option expiration commonly occurs some time before the expiration of the underlying futures contract for the reason of managing exercised options into futures. Not always, however, there are some markets where they expire on the very same day.

When an option is exercised, it is offset from your account and a futures position from the strike price of the option is placed in the account in place of the option. The expiration date is often available on quote systems and will be displayed with the quote information. It is handy to have a commodity expiration calendar or commodity specifications sheet to determine exact expiration dates for each option. You can usually obtain exact expiration dates from your broker or adviser as well. In Figure 2-2 we have an example of a commodity expiration calendar, showing option expirations for one week.

These calendars are also handy because they often show the dates of significant market reports, futures expirations, and market holidays.

24	25	26	27	28
OE: Jan DAX Options-EUREX OE: Jan DJ EURO STOXX 50 Options-EUREX OE: Jan DJ EURO STOXX Sector Index Options-EUREX OE: Jan DJ STOXX 50 Options-EUREX OE: Jan Euro Bobl-EUREX OE: Jan Euro Bund-EUREX		OE: Feb Aluminum-CMX OE: Feb Copper-CMX OE: Feb Gasoline-NY Unleaded-NYM OE: Feb Gold-CMX OE: Feb Heating Oil-NYM OE: Feb Natural Gas H. Hub-NYM OE: Feb Silver-CMX		OE: Jan Cattle-Feeder Options-CME OE: Jan Hang Seng Index-HKEX OE: Jan MSCI TAIWAN-SGX

FIGURE 2-2
Expiration Calendar

CALLS AND PUTS

Now that we understand the definition of an option and what options are, we can look at the two types of options.

Call Options A call option is the right to purchase, or go long, the underlying futures contract at specified price and at a specified point in time. Figure 2-1 shows a listing of call options. If a call option is exercised into the underlying future, the option holder will be long the underlying futures contact at the strike price of the option. Let's look at Figure 2-1 again.

Contract	Open	High	Low	Bid	Ask	Last
C-H05,C150						20092
C-H05,C160						2
C-H05,C170						1
C-H05,C180		247	247			247
C-H05,C190	136	157	136		136	157
C-H05,C200	80	85	70		72	85
C-H05,C205	26	26	26			26
C-H05,C210	40	43	34	40	35	43
C-H05,C215				15		
C-H05,C220	20	21	15	17	16	21
C-H05,C230	10	11	7	10	10	10
C-H05,C240	10	4	3	4		4
C-H05,C250	4	4	2	2	3	2

FIGURE 2-1

A 220 strike price March corn call would give the option holder the right, but not the obligation, to purchase the underlying March corn futures at 220.

Put Options A put option is the right, but not the obligation, to sell (or short), the underlying futures contract at a specified price and at a specified point in time.

In Figure 2-3 you see a sample of the symbol, commodity, and strike price for March corn put options. A March corn 220 put would give the holder the right to sell, or short, the December corn futures at 220. A 200 put would give the holder the right, but not the obligation, to sell the underlying futures at 200.

Contract	Open	High	Low	Bid	Ask	Last	PClose
C-H05,P160		1	1			1	1
C-H05,P170	1	1	1			1	1
C-H05,P180	3	3	2	2	3	2	2
C-H05,P185		3	3			3	3
C-H05,P190	3	14	11	12		11	11
C-H05,P195	30	30	21			21	21
C-H05,P200	44	52	37	50	42	37	37
C-H05,P205	72	72	63			63	63
C-H05,P210	102	114	94		100	94	94
C-H05,P220	180	192	171	186	184	171	171
C-H05,P230	276	284	260		270	260	260
C-H05,P240		354	354			354	354
C-H05,P250		453	453			453	453

FIGURE 2-3
March corn puts

TEST YOUR KNOWLEDGE 2-1

1. An option is an obligation to the underlying futures. True or False?
2. The strike price is the price at which an option may be exercised into the underlying future. True or False?
3. The option expiration date is the date at which the underlying future changes to an option. True or False?
4. A 500 soybean put would have the right, but not the obligation, to be _____ the underlying futures at 500.
5. A _____ contains the expiration and contract information.

MARKET QUOTES AND OPTION PREMIUM

The page or listing you see in Figure 2-1 would be referred to as a *quote page* or *option chain*. The method of the quote depends on the individual market and the system creating the quote. In Figure 2-1, the options traded price in the column marked "Last" is called the *option's premium*. An option's premium is the

Contract	Open	High	Low	Bid	Ask	Last
C-H05,C150						20092
C-H05,C160						2
C-H05,C170						1
C-H05,C180		247	247			247
C-H05,C190	136	157	136		136	157
C-H05,C200	80	85	70		72	85
C-H05,C205	26	26	26			26
C-H05,C210	40	43	34	40	35	43
C-H05,C215				15		
C-H05,C220	20	21	15	17	16	21
C-H05,C230	10	11	7	10	10	10
C-H05,C240	10	4	3	4		4
C-H05,C250	4	4	2	2	3	2

FIGURE 2-1

determination of the option's value and the price at which the option has most recently traded. If we look at the Last price for the March 200 call option, we see an 85. In the case of this option it means 8 ⅝ because the grain options are quoted in 8ths. The last digit is the fraction and the remaining numbers are whole points. The March 190 call option shows 157 in the Last column. This would mean 15 ⅞. How the quote should be read varies with each market and quote provider. In this book you'll see several different examples of quote methods and different markets to help you understand what to look for when looking up option prices.

Options, like futures, are traded on the floor of the exchange, usually side by side with the underlying futures contract in a section of the pit. Options are also traded in an open outcry, bid-and-offer format like their futures counterparts (electronic markets are done by computers matching bids and offers).

Bid—a trader's willing price to purchase a futures or option contract.

Offer—a trader's willing price to sell a futures or option contract.

You can see in Figure 2-1, the columns marked for bid and ask (this is the offer price). When making a bid for an option contract, you are bidding on the premium of the option, not the strike price or the futures price. The ability to purchase an option depends on the willingness of someone to sell an option at the premium you are bidding. If your bid for an option contract is accepted, you then own the contract and must have the funds in your trading account for the dollar amount of the premium. The bids and offers for the trading session determine the option's premium and settlement for the session. This premium value is what will be reflected in your account as the daily value of your option position.

The fluctuation of option premium or value is related in many ways to the movement of the underlying futures contract. However, since options are traded independently, the futures fluctuation in value may or may not be reflected in the option premium each day. Options also tend to trade less frequently and have lower open interest or number of contracts open, which can account for many intraday or day-to-day discrepancies in valuation.

"THE MONEY"

There are three very important terms that you will hear when discussing options.

At the Money— This term means that the strike price of the option is in very close proximity to the current futures price.

In the Money— This term refers to options for which the underlying futures price has surpassed the option's strike price in the direction of the option.

Out of the money— This term refers to options for which the underlying futures price has not yet reached the strike price of the option. Again this would be in the direction of the option, call versus put.

In Figure 2-4 we use the December 2002 corn call options with a little different quote method. For the December 2002 corn futures at 260 you can see the in-the-money options highlighted in dark gray, at-the-money options in white, and out-of-the-money options in light gray.

In the next example, Figure 2-5, we use the December 2002 corn put options. The December 2002 corn market is at 220, figure out which options here are in the money, at the money, and out of the money.

Check your answers with Figure 2-6 below. You should have noted the put options with strike prices below 220 as out of the money, the 220 strike as at the money, and the strike prices above 220 as in the money.

Symbol	Name	Str	Last	ExpDate
CCCZ02210	Corn	210	24'2	11/23/02
CCCZ02220	Corn	220	19'0	11/23/02
CCCZ02230	Corn	230	14'5	11/23/02
CCCZ02240	Corn	240	11'2	11/23/02
CCCZ02250	Corn	250	8'6	11/23/02
CCCZ02260	Corn	260	At the Money 2	
CCCZ02270	Corn	270	5'2	11/23/02
CCCZ02280	Corn	280	4'1	11/23/02
CCCZ02290	Corn	290	3'2	11/23/02
CCCZ02300	Corn	300	2'5	11/23/02

In the Money

Out of the Money

At the Money

FIGURE 2-4
The money

Symbol	Name	Str	Last	ExpDate
PCCZ02200	Corn	200	5'5	11/23/02
PCCZ02210	Corn	210	9'4	11/23/02
PCCZ02220	Corn	220	14'4	11/23/02
PCCZ02230	Corn	230	20'4	11/23/02
PCCZ02240	Corn	240	27'3	11/23/02
PCCZ02250	Corn	250	35'0	11/23/02
PCCZ02260	Corn	260	43'2	11/23/02

FIGURE 2-5
In, out, at the money

Symbol	Name	Str	Last	ExpDate
PCCZ02200	Corn	200	5'5	11/23/02
PCCZ02210	Corn	210	9'4	11/23/02
PCCZ02220	Corn	220	At the money	11/23/02
PCCZ02230	Corn	230	20'4	11/23/02
PCCZ02240	Corn	240	27'3	11/23/02
PCCZ02250	Corn	250	35'0	11/23/02
PCCZ02260	Corn	260	43'2	11/23/02

Out of the Money

At the money

In the Money

FIGURE 2-6
The money answer

TEST YOUR KNOWLEDGE 2-2

1. An option's price is called premium. True or False?
2. An option's premium moves the same as the underlying futures all the time. True or False?
3. If the soybean market is now at 475, then the 480 call would be in the money. True or False? A 1500 cocoa call option would be _____ if the futures were at 1490.
4. Options tend to trade _____ frequently than the underlying futures contract.

OPTION VALUE: INTRINSIC VERSUS TIME

An option has two basic value components which make up the option's premium.

Intrinsic Value Intrinsic value is present in options that are in the money. This value is related to the option's strike price and the current futures price when the option is in the money.

- A call option has intrinsic value when the futures price is higher than the strike price of the option.

   Example: If the Nov Soybean futures market is at 475, then the 450 call would have 25 cents of intrinsic value in the premium.

- A put option has intrinsic value when the futures price is lower than the strike price of the option.

   Example: If the Sep Silver futures market is at 460, than the 480 put would have 20 cents intrinsic value.

Time Value This is sometimes referred to as *risk value. Time value* represents the premium above intrinsic value. If the option has no intrinsic value, then the entire premium is time value. Time value is the portion of the value associated with the risk of selling the option. In other words, the seller of the option is collecting time value for his or her risk of selling the option on the market.

- Out-of-the-money and at-the-money option premium is typically entirely time value, having no intrinsic value.

Typically, options with more time till expiration have more risk of market change; therefore, they have more time value.

Let's look at Figure 2-7 and determine what is time value and what is intrinsic value. In this figure we have highlighted the December 2002 corn futures as the underlying futures contract. Also notice that we have now added the column DTE, which represents the days till expiration of each contract. Notice the shorter expiration of the option versus the underlying futures contract.

In Figure 2-7 we have the December futures at a settlement price of 229'4, or 229 ½, and the December corn 220 call at 20. If the market is at 229 ½ and it's a 220 call, then we have 9 1/2 cents of intrinsic value.

Use this formula for call options:

$$\text{Futures Price} - \text{Strike Price} = \text{Intrinsic Value}$$

$$229\ \tfrac{1}{2} - 220 = 9\ \tfrac{1}{2}$$

Now let's look at how much time value this example has:

$$\text{Option Premium} - \text{Intrinsic Value} = \text{Time Value}$$

$$20 - 9\ \tfrac{1}{2} = 10\ \tfrac{1}{2}$$

Our next example, Figure 2-8, is the same December 2002 corn underlying futures contract only now using a put option that is just very slightly in the money.

In Figure 2-8 we have the December futures at a settlement price of 229'4, or 229 ½, again and the December corn 230 put at 15'7, or 15 7/8. If the market is at 229 ½ and it's a 230 put, then we have ½ cent of intrinsic value.

Symbol	Name	Str	Last	DTE	ExpDate
CZ02	Corn (Day)	0	229'4	194	12/13/02
CCCZ02220	Corn	220	20'0	174	11/23/02

FIGURE 2-7
December corn

Symbol	Name	Str	Last	DTE	ExpDate
CZ02	Corn (Day)	0	229'4	194	12/13/02
PCCZ02230	Corn	230	15'7	174	11/23/02

FIGURE 2-8
December corn put

Use this formula for put options:

$$\text{Strike Price} - \text{Futures Price} = \text{Intrinsic Value}$$

$$230 - 229\,\tfrac{1}{2} = \tfrac{1}{2}$$

Now let's look at how much time value this example has:

$$\text{Option Premium} - \text{Intrinsic Value} = \text{Time Value}$$

$$15\,\tfrac{7}{8} - \tfrac{1}{2} = 15\,\tfrac{3}{8}$$

TIME VALUE AND TIME DECAY

Time Value is one of the major features of risk when trading options. An options time value decreases from the option's inception to the date of expiration. This loss of value we call *time decay.* In Figure 2-9, we have a new example using the September 2002, 30-year U.S. Treasury bond. This contract is ideal for demonstration because it has two serial options in between the underlying futures contract, which is highlighted. By using three options on the same underlying futures contract, we can easily assess time decay without significant effect from futures basis or futures volatility.

The column that was labeled "Last" in the previous examples is shown here as "OlSet" (SETTLE on varying quote systems). It represents the previous day's or today's settlement of the premium, respectively. We also have a column here labeled "Theta," which will be discussed further on. We have selected three options at the same strike price but from different contract months. In this case we are using July, August, and September. You can also see that the premium of these options reflects the increased time value. The intrinsic value is the same

Symbol	Name	Str	OlSet	Theta	DTE	ExpDate
USU02	US Treasury Bo	0	101'09		109	9/19/02
CUSN021010	US Treasury Bo	1010	1'11	1.51	20	6/22/02
CUSQ021010	US Treasury Bo	1010	1'50	0.92	55	7/27/02
CUSU021010	US Treasury Bo	1010	2'09	0.73	83	8/24/02

FIGURE 2-9
September U.S. Treasury

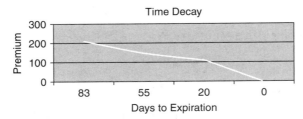

FIGURE 2-10
Time decay

on each option because the strike price is the same on each; therefore, the distance from the underlying future is the same. The July option, having only 20 days until expiration, has a lower premium than the farther or deferred August and September option contracts.

Figure 2-10 shows the options and the rate of decay. The rate of decay is expressed in the column labeled "Theta" in Figure 2-9. Time value tends to remain fairly stable from 100 remaining days until 45 or so. You can see that the time decay begins to accelerate rapidly toward day 0 when no time value exists.

Theta values increase from 0. The formula for theta is somewhat complicated, but essentially, the higher the value the faster the time decay rate. Understanding the rate of time value decay is important when buying or selling options. Buyers need to understand the potential rate of premium loss. The higher the

---

TEST YOUR KNOWLEDGE 2-3

1. Intrinsic value represents the entire option premium. True or False?
2. Time value tends to decay from the inception of the option till the date of expiration. True or False?
3. Time decay tends to be more rapid as an option nears expiration. True or False?
4. A 1500 cocoa call with the underlying futures trading at 1490 would have _____ intrinsic value.
5. A 1500 cocoa call with the underlying futures at 1590 would have _____ intrinsic value?

theta, the more the risk of premium loss increases. Sellers benefit from faster decay, and decreasing option value.

We will discuss time decay more in your strategies later in the book. The best method to utilized theta in your trading is to get the information from a quote system or from your broker. Most brokers have this information in option analysis software. You can also find simple option calculators available online as stand-alone software or for Excel-type programs if you are interested in building your own option model program.

IMPLIED VOLATILITY

You will hear the term *implied volatility* used repeatedly throughout the industry. Traders commonly refer to implied volatility when discussing futures and options markets. We are going to try to bring the complexities of this terminology to a simple usable methodology for your trading, rather than a long discussion of calculations.

First we can again say that the best place to find implied volatility is an option calculator or your broker. When you are trading or evaluating a trade strategy, it is beneficial to have this information, as you will see in later chapters.

Implied volatility simply is a measure of the strike price and premium of an option in relation to the underlying futures price. Even more simply, it's a measure of supply and demand for an option.

Implied volatility shows us when an option has increased or decreased in value versus the underlying futures price. This happens when demand for an option rises or falls.

Here is an example: Let's say that hypothetically traders are interested in buying a particular call or group of call options because of an impending government report, the premium of those options may rise disproportionately to the normal movement of the option versus that day's futures movement. This would represent an increase in implied volatility. Now let's say the report comes out bearish. The extra premium bid into the group of calls would likely evaporate quickly as traders exit positions following the report. This would cause the implied volatility to fall

Figure 2-11 shows you how implied volatility is quoted on a group of options. You can see a new column in the figure "ImpVol." This is the quote for

Symbol	Str	OISet	ImpVol	DTE	ExpDate
CSSQ02440	440	65'0	0.2499	52	7/27/02
CSSQ02460	460	47'5	0.2448	52	7/27/02
CSSQ02480	480	33'5	0.2509	52	7/27/02
CSSQ02500	500	23'0	0.2645	52	7/27/02
CSSQ02520	520	15'2	0.2761	52	7/27/02
CSSQ02540	540	10'2	0.2892	52	7/27/02
CSSQ02560	560	7'0	0.3019	52	7/27/02
CSSQ02580	580	4'6	0.3198	52	7/27/02
CSSQ02600	600	3'1	0.3309	52	7/27/02
CSSQ02620	620	2'2	0.3450	52	7/27/02
CSSQ02640	640	1'5	0.3686	52	7/27/02
CSSQ02680	680	0'7	0.3922	52	7/27/02
CSSQ02700	700	0'6	0.4120	52	7/27/02

FIGURE 2-11
August soybean calls

implied volatility and is shown as a percentage or decimal. Lower numbers equal lower volatility, higher numbers equal increased volatility. Out–of-the-money options traditionally have higher implied volatility than options that are at the money or in the money; although in markets where the anticipated range is very limited, you will see implied volatility fall sharply due to lack of demand for out-of-the-money options.

Figure 2-12 shows how implied volatility varies from commodity to commodity. Each commodity future has its own average and historical volatility. A volatility of 25% may be extremely high for one commodity and extremely low for another. The best reference for average volatility for each commodity is to locate a historical volatility database or source to compare current levels with historical averages. This information is also typically available from your broker and there are many online resources.

The advantage of utilizing implied volatility in your trading is to capitalize on undervalued options when implied volatility is low and avoid overspending on premium when volatility is high. Implied volatility analysis is the first tool for the option seller, looking for overvalued premium. You'll learn more about implied volatility in buying and selling options in Chapters 3 through 6.

Three cautions about implied volatility analysis:

Symbol	Str	OISet	ImpVol	DTE	ExpDate
CCCZ02200	200	30'2	0.2315	171	11/23/02
CCCZ02210	210	23'4	0.2346	171	11/23/02
CCCZ02220	220	18'0	0.2316	171	11/23/02
CCCZ02230	230	13'3	0.2357	171	11/23/02
CCCZ02240	240	10'1	0.2458	171	11/23/02
CCCZ02250	250	7'7	0.2524	171	11/23/02
CCCZ02260	260	6'0	0.2611	171	11/23/02
CCCZ02270	270	4'5	0.2706	171	11/23/02
CCCZ02280	280	3'5	0.2777	171	11/23/02
CCCZ02290	290	2'7	0.2843	171	11/23/02

FIGURE 2-12
December corn calls

- Implied volatility is a past-tense indicator from the most recent futures trade and option premium. Sometimes this can be only a few seconds or sometimes it can be settlement a day earlier. This indication from the last trade or settlement may not be representative of the next trade or settlement.
- Options are a bid-offer market, the implied volatility you see may not be current with the floor bid and offer.
- Implied volatility can remain outside of normal ranges for some time; it is not necessarily an indication of an impending change.

OPTION DELTA

Another major piece of the option puzzle is an analysis tool called *delta*. Delta is a mathematical formula for option analysis included in a group of formulas the industry calls *Greeks*. The theta we discussed previously is in this group.

As we mentioned previously, options do not necessarily move directly with the underlying futures contract. We measure the relationship between an option's price change to the price change in the underlying futures with the formula delta. Delta is defined as the expression of the rate change between an option and the underlying futures contract. This rate is expressed in a decimal or percentage of 1.00, which is always the delta of a futures contract. In other words, if an option has a delta of .50 or 50%, you might expect the option's premium to change 50% of the futures price change for the day.

First let's look at why options move only a portion of the futures movement. In Figure 2-13 we have added hypothetical delta figures to simplify things a bit. The underlying futures contract is highlighted, showing a delta of 1.00.

Figure 2-13 shows the at-the-money option with a delta of 50%. As you move in the money, the delta of the options continues to increase. As you move out of the money, the delta of the options gradually decreases. This delta scale is created by the risk factor of the option seller. Options that are in the money have intrinsic value that increases or decreases with each tick of the futures contract. The more intrinsic value it has, the greater the risk to the option seller that the contract will emulate the underlying futures contract in a move against the seller's position. Option strike prices that are farther from the current market have less immediate risk to the option seller so bid and offers will reflect less of the immediate futures movement. Typically, at-the-money options will be at or near 50% delta, in the money options greater than 50% and out-of-the-money options less than 50%.

Remember, all of this is created by evaluation of risk by those buying and selling. The trade creates the delta, not the other way around. Now let's look at an actual example captured from market trade. Figure 2-14 shows the actual delta figures of August 2002 soybean call options from 440 to 700. Look at the figure to see if you can tell where the underlying futures contract might be trading. Hint: Look for the at-the-money option delta.

The market capture for this graphic was actually around 506 making the 500 call slightly in the money; however, we would consider this option to be at the money.

Symbol	Name	Str	Delta	DTE	ExpDate
CSSQ02460	Soybeans	460	.90	53	7/27/02
CSSQ02480	Soybeans	480	.70	53	7/27/02
CSSQ02500	Soybeans	500	.50	53	7/27/02
SQ02	Soybeans (Day)	0	1.00	71	8/14/02
CSSQ02520	Soybeans	520	.40	53	7/27/02
CSSQ02540	Soybeans	540	.30	53	7/27/02
CSSQ02560	Soybeans	560	.20	53	7/27/02

FIGURE 2-13
August soybean combined

Symbol	Str	Delta	DTE	ExpDate
CSSQ02440	440	0.9302	52	7/27/02
CSSQ02460	460	0.8544	52	7/27/02
CSSQ02480	480	0.7244	52	7/27/02
CSSQ02500	500	0.5663	52	7/27/02
CSSQ02520	520	0.4171	52	7/27/02
CSSQ02540	540	0.2948	52	7/27/02
CSSQ02560	560	0.2032	52	7/27/02
CSSQ02580	580	0.1428	52	7/27/02
CSSQ02600	600	0.0970	52	7/27/02
CSSQ02620	620	0.0678	52	7/27/02
CSSQ02640	640	0.0530	52	7/27/02
CSSQ02680	680	0.0275	52	7/27/02
CSSQ02700	700	0.0224	52	7/27/02

FIGURE 2-14
August soybean calls

Put options will look similar; however, most typically there are fewer put strike prices actively traded than call strike prices. We will apply delta frequently in Chapters 3 through 6.

TEST YOUR KNOWLEDGE 2-4

1. Implied volatility is a potential measure of supply and demand for options. True or False?

2. Implied volatility is an average of 25% on commodity futures. True or False?

3. Delta gives an indication of how an option's premium will change when the futures price changes. True or False?

4. The at-the-money option usually has a _____ delta.

5. Put options often have _____ trading strike prices than call options.

KEY TERMS

At-the-money Options in which the underlying future is near or at the strike price.

Bid The premium at which a trader is willing to buy the option contract.

Call option The right, but not the obligation, to buy or be long the underlying futures contract.

Delta The representation of the percentage of change in price between an option and the underlying futures contract.

Expiration date The date on which an option must be either exercised into the underlying futures contract or be allowed to expire without value.

Implied volatility The measure of the strike price and premium of an option in relation to the underlying futures price. A measure of supply and demand for an option.

In the money Options in which the underlying future has surpassed the strike price.

Intrinsic value Actual option value. Only in-the-money options have intrinsic value.

Offer The premium at which a trader is willing to sell the option contract.

Option The right, but not the obligation, to the underlying futures contract at a specific price and specific point in time.

Out of the money Options in which the underlying future is away from the strike price.

Premium The price or value of the option contract.

Put option The right, but not the obligation, to sell or be short the underlying futures contract.

Serial option An option contract without the same month underlying futures contract. These options typically trade off the next closest futures contract.

Strike price The price at which an option can be exercised into the underlying futures contract.

Theta The representation of the rate of time value decay for an option.

Time value The risk value or trading value of an option on top of intrinsic value. If no intrinsic value exists, the entire premium is time value.

CHAPTER TEST

1. In the definition of an option, "at a specific price" refers to a?
   - (a) Premium
   - (b) Settlement
   - (c) Strike price
   - (d) All of the above

2. The right, but not the obligation, to be long the underlying futures is called a?
   - (a) Warrant
   - (b) Call
   - (c) Put
   - (d) Theta

3. An option without a same month underlying futures contract is called a/an?
   - (a) Small option
   - (b) Odd option
   - (c) Delta option
   - (d) Serial option

4. The price you pay for an option is called a/an?
   - (a) Strike price
   - (b) Premium
   - (c) Implied value
   - (d) Gamma

5. Which of the following options has intrinsic value?
   - (a) At-the-money option
   - (b) In-the-money option
   - (c) Out-of-the-money option
   - (d) None

6. An out-of-the-money option does not have which of the following?
   - (a) Delta
   - (b) Premium

        (c) Intrinsic value

        (d) Time value

   7. Which of the following describes the reason for time decay?

        (a) Traders bid less for options because there is less time for opportunity.

        (b) As expiration approaches futures, fundamentals may be more predictable.

        (c) Option sellers stop selling 30 days before expiration.

        (d) a and b only

   8. Which of the following is the correct formula for finding intrinsic value in a call option?

        (a) Strike Price – Futures Price = Intrinsic Value

        (b) Futures Price – Strike Price = Intrinsic Value

   9. Implied volatility is a measure of what?

        (a) Time decay

        (b) Futures price

        (c) Option demand

        (d) All of the above

  10. Which of the following options would likely have a 54% delta if the futures market was at 494?

        (a) 490 put

        (b) 500 call

        (c) 490 call

        (d) 480 put

ANSWERS TO TESTS

Test Your Knowledge 2-1

1. False. Remember the definition of an option: An option is a right, but not an obligation. 2. True. The strike price represents the price at which the option may be exercised into the underlying futures. 3. False. A little trick question, the expiration date is the date at which an option must be exercised into the

underlying future or the option will expire. 4. Short. 5. commodity expiration calendar

Test Your Knowledge 2-2

1. True. The trades made on the floor represent the premium of the option. 2. False. There are many factors involved in the traded premium of an option position; rarely will options ever move exactly with the underlying futures contract. 3. False. If the soybean market is at 475, then only calls below 475 would be in the money. 4. Out of the Money. 5. Loss.

Test Your Knowledge 2-3

1. False. Intrinsic value represents only the portion of the option premium which is considered in the money premium. 2. True. Remember, the time value is the risk value; the longer the term, the more risk to the seller. 3. True. As an option nears expiration time decay tends to accelerate; remember to watch the theta value. 4. 0 (zero). 5. 90 (1590 − 1500 = 90).

Test Your Knowledge 2-4

1. True. Implied volatility is an indicator that shows when premiums change against the underlying futures contract, which can be an indication of demand. 2. False. Implied volatility varies from commodity to commodity. 3. False. Delta is the measure of the price change of an option versus the price change of the underlying future. 4. 50%. 5. fewer.

Chapter Test

1. c. The strike price is the expression of the price at which the option can be exercised into the underlying futures.

2. b. The right to be long the market comes from a call option.

3. d. Serial options do not have an underlying futures contract in the same calendar month.

4. b. The premium represents the current value of an option and is also the traded price of the option.

5. b. Only in-the-money options have intrinsic value; this value is actual value from the distance of the strike price to the current underlying futures trade.

6. c. Out-of-the-money options have no intrinsic value.

7. d. The future is more predictable with less time, and short option risk decreases as less market range is likely.

8. a. Strike Price – Futures Price = Intrinsic Value

9. c. Option demand or supply

10. c. The 490 call is slightly in the money and would likely have a delta greater than 50%.

CHAPTER 3

BUYING AND SELLING OPTIONS

We will now begin buying and selling options. In this chapter we will cover:

- The basics of buying options
- Buying call options
- Buying put options
- Calculating purchased option breakeven
- Liquidating purchased options
- The basics of selling options
- Selling call options
- Selling put options
- Calculating breakeven on sold options
- Liquidating options

BUYING OPTIONS

The first thing to learn about trading options is the basics of buying and selling individual options. There are several advantages to buying individual options:

Limited or Defined Risk When you purchase an option your risk on that option is limited to the premium which you have spent on the option plus the costs of trading, such as commissions and fees.

Margin When you purchase an option you are paying the premium of the option up front when you enter the trade, so no matter the futures movement the option will not demand additional margin deposits unless the option were to expire in the money and be exercised into the underlying futures. At that point you should expect margin from the futures contract.

Multiple Positions Many traders will select out-of-the-money options with low premium and purchase multiple positions to increase opportunity. We'll cover more of this strategy's advantages and risks.

Leverage Sometimes at-the-money option premium will require less initial cost (lower premium) than the initial futures margin. Although, the call option will only perform according to the delta instead of moving directly with the futures price. This would also be the case when considering buying out-of-the-money options. Option strike prices that are farther from the current market tend to have lower premium costs.

Unlimited Potential The other very significant advantage to outright purchased options is the potential for unlimited performance with limited risk. Put options are technically limited in gain potential because a commodity price cannot fall below zero.

There are also disadvantages to buying options:

Time Decay This is the primary risk factor when considering buying options. As we've discussed, time value decreases from the day the option opens for trade to the day the option expires. Time value is a continuous risk and options are a depreciating asset. Later we will discuss methods of managing time value risk.

Liquidity As we have discussed, this can be a risk of any market transaction whether it be futures or options. However, because there are a large number of strike prices typically with each underlying futures contract, the market interest is spread across many contracts. This can leave certain strike prices with only a few open positions at any one time. This is especially true in markets that have low volume conditions in the underlying futures.

Volatility Market conditions which cause volatility in the underlying futures typically do the same to the implied volatility of the related options. Now this can be an advantage or disadvantage depending on your current position; acquiring new option positions at higher volatility can expose the position to the risk of premium decay from decreasing volatility as well as time value decay. If the demand that created the volatility evaporates after you purchase the option and volatility falls, so will your premium, making your option worth less aside from any movement in the underlying futures

Symbol	Str	OISet	ImpVol	Delta	DTE	ExpDate
CCCZ02200	200	30'0	0.2315	0.7858	171	11/23/02
CCCZ02210	210	23'2	0.2346	0.6919	171	11/23/02
CCCZ02220	220	17'2	0.2316	0.5896	171	11/23/02
CCCZ02230	230	12'6	0.2357	0.4832	171	11/23/02
CCCZ02240	240	9'5	0.2458	0.3889	171	11/23/02
CCCZ02250	250	7'1	0.2524	0.3074	171	11/23/02
CCCZ02260	260	5'3	0.2611	0.2426	171	11/23/02
CCCZ02270	270	4'1	0.2706	0.1922	171	11/23/02
CCCZ02280	280	3'1	0.2777	0.1508	171	11/23/02
CCCZ02290	290	2'3	0.2843	0.1183	171	11/23/02

FIGURE 3-1
December corn calls

BUYING CALLS

Buying call options is the most common option trade. When you purchase a call option you are paying for the right to purchase, or be long, the underlying futures at the strike price of the option as in our definition of an option.

Let's look at selecting a call option to purchase in Figure 3-1 and calculate the premium costs in dollars.

In Figure 3-1, look at the highlighted purchase of the 230 call option. The settlement price quoted for the 230 call is 12'6 or 12¾.

The corn contract represented is 5000 bushels and the option price is in cents per bushel. The calculation below shows the size and the option price multiplied together to get the actual cost in U.S. dollars.

$$5000bu \times 0.1275 = \$637.50$$

Let's try another one, the December corn 270 call price shown is

$$4'1 (4\ 1/8) = 0.04125$$

$$5000bu \times 0.04125 = \$206.25$$

Look at another example from the live cattle market in Figure 3-2. See if you can calculate the price. Live Cattle is a 40,000-lb contract.

In Figure 3-2 we have purchased an August Live Cattle 6400 at 1.100. The maximum risk on this position is the purchased premium of 1.10 plus whatever

Symbol	Str	OlSet	ImpVol	Delta	DTE	ExpDate
CLCQ026000	6000	3.175	0.2192	0.5990	58	8/2/02
CLCQ026100	6100	2.600	0.2145	0.5253	58	8/2/02
CLCQ026200	6200	2.000	0.2122	0.4495	58	8/2/02
CLCQ026300	6300	1.550	0.1909	0.3604	58	8/2/02
CLCQ026400	6400	1.100	0.1904	0.2861	58	8/2/02

Live Cattle is a 40,000lb contract. Quotes are in cents/pound/hundred. The calculation is then
$40000 \times .01100 = \$440$

FIGURE 3-2
August live cattle calls

cost and fees of trading you may be charged. Now that we have this option, let's look at how we would gain or lose on a purchased call option. Remember, a call is the right, but not the obligation, to be long the futures. So, in order for the value of an option to rise we must see an increase in the underlying futures price causing the premium of the option contract to rise.

Figure 3-3 is an option model of our cattle call purchase. In the model you will notice that the horizontal axis is the underlying futures price and the vertical axis is the option premium. You will first notice the light gray horizontal line being the option purchase premium at 1.10. The dark gray line represents the value of the option on the expiration date in comparison to the underlying futures price. The thin gray line is entirely hypothetical; however it is a fairly accurate representation of the value of the option in the short term, incorporating time value into the premium. Now take a look at the dark gray expiration line and you will notice that the premium is entirely intrinsic value. Going back to the thin gray line, let's assume that the futures price moves quickly, assuming little or no time decay. What might the option premium be if the futures price moved to 66.00? Probably around 2.50 or so. If we were to sell the 64.00 call at that point we would have a profit of 1.40 minus fees and cost of trading

2.50(value at offset) − 1.10(purchase price)
= 1.40 profit, or $560 minus cost of trading

Should the underlying futures price fall, you can see that the option premium would likely get progressively worse being affected by time decay as well as the

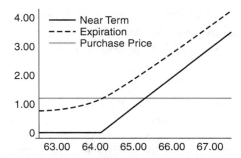

FIGURE 3-3
Cattle option model

loss of value. If the futures market is at or below the strike price and you hold the option to expiration, the premium will be 0. If the option was sold in the short term with the underlying futures at 63.00, there would be a loss of premium. Looking back at the model we can see that the premium hypothetically might be 0.70 which would equate to

$$1.10 - 0.70 = 0.40 \text{ loss, or } \$160 \text{ loss plus cost of trading}$$

If the underlying futures price falls and stays below the strike price (line values to the left of the purchase price) for enough time, the option premium will eventually fall to a zero bid value which the market calls *cab* (cabinet bid). The premium is eliminated completely at expiration and the entire premium plus costs of trading are lost.

Let's look at one more example using Figure 3-2. Let's try buying the 6100 strike price at 2.60. The option premium in dollars is going to calculate to

$$40,000 \text{lbs} \times 0.0260 = \$1040$$

If the market were to rise, and the premium increased to 3.20, what would the premium taken back in be?

$$40,000 \times 0320 = \$1280$$

The option would be sold for $1280, but we have to subtract the initial premium paid to calculate our net profit.

$$\$1280 - \$1040 = \$240 \text{ minus costs of trading}$$

Remember, buying calls is the right, but not the obligation, to be long the underlying futures contract. Buying calls is the most common option trade because it is human nature to want investments or prices to rise in value; but remember when buying a call option, the market has to rise for the option to gain value. Look for markets that are likely to do just that.

BUYING PUTS

When you purchase a put option you are paying for the right to sell, or be short, the underlying futures at the strike price of the option as in our definition of an option.

Let's look at purchasing a put option as we did with the call option.

In Figure 3-4 we show the purchase of the December corn 220 put at 10 ¾. The calculation of premium here is the same as the call option purchase earlier.

$$5000bu \times 0.1075 = \$537.50$$

With the purchase of the put option, remember we are purchasing the right to be short the underlying futures contract. So, in order for the put option position to gain in value, the underlying futures contract will have to move toward the option strike price or to a farther in-the-money price to gain option premium value. In this case, if the corn futures contract falls toward the strike price or even falls far enough to be in the money, then the option value will likely increase.

Looking at the premium of this option as we did on the call option, if we were to sell the option at a premium of 22 ¾, we would have a profit of

$$22 \text{ ¾} - 10 \text{ ¾} = 12 \text{ cents per bushel}$$

Symbol	Str	OISet	ImpVol	Delta	DTE	ExpDate
PCCZ02190	190	1'7	0.2229	0.1054	171	11/23/02
PCCZ02200	200	3'5	0.2225	0.1789	171	11/23/02
PCCZ02210	210	6'6	0.2305	0.2780	171	11/23/02
PCCZ02220	220	10'6	0.2327	0.3829	171	11/23/02
PCCZ02230	230	16'2	0.2413	0.4875	171	11/23/02
PCCZ02240	240	22'4	0.2456	0.5835	171	11/23/02
PCCZ02250	250	30'1	0.2597	0.6585	171	11/23/02

FIGURE 3-4
December corn puts

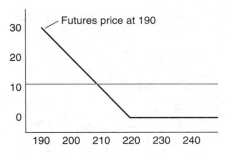

FIGURE 3-5
Corn option model

$$0.12 = 5000 = \$600$$

Now we always want to keep in mind that time value and implied volatility come into play as to what the potential future premium value of the put option may be. Remember that the option only has real value or intrinsic value when it is in the money; the balance is all time value.

Let's look at the option model in Figure 3-5 to see the intrinsic value of the option versus various futures prices.

The horizontal axis in Figure 3-5 has the futures price of the Dec corn contract, while the vertical has premium value. We show intrinsic value only at expiration with the thick gray line. The option's premium is at zero until the futures price falls to 220. Descending from 220 the option premium increases with the top of the line showing at the 30-cent mark. The underlying future is priced at 190 at this point. Above the 220 mark you can see that the option value falls eventually to zero.

This means a total loss of purchase option premium and cost of trading. If the option is not yet to expiration any value above 0 when the futures market is above 220 would be time value. Time value decay would reduce this value to zero at expiration. The horizontal line on this graphic is of course our purchase price.

Let's look at another example of a put option in a different market in Figure 3-6 and see if you can draw the model and calculate how much premium there would be at certain futures prices. Get a piece of scratch paper to work with.

In Figure 3-6 we are showing the purchase of the August lean hog 44 put at a premium of 2.05. Lean hogs is a 40,000 lb contract so each

$$40,000 \times 0.0205 = \$820.00$$

Symbol	Str	OISet	ImpVol	Delta	DTE	ExpDate
PLHQ023600	3600	0.400	0.4279	0.0817	87	8/31/02
PLHQ023800	3800	0.600	0.4081	0.1189	87	8/31/02
PLHQ024000	4000	0.900	0.4005	0.1742	87	8/31/02
PLHQ024200	4200	1.450	0.3812	0.2376	87	8/31/02
PLHQ024400	4400	2.050	0.3705	0.3179	87	8/31/02
PLHQ024600	4600	2.900	0.3633	0.4086	87	8/31/02
PLHQ024800	4800	3.950	0.3633	0.5023	87	8/31/02
PLHQ025000	5000	5.200	0.3626	0.5921	87	8/31/02
PLHQ025200	5200	6.575	0.3574	0.6768	87	8/31/02
PLHQ025400	5400	8.150	0.3665	0.7412	87	8/31/02

FIGURE 3-6
August lean hog put

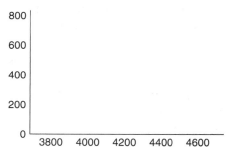

FIGURE 3-7
Blank model

We now have the right, but not the obligation, to be short the underlying futures contract which in this case is the August lean hogs at 44.00 or 44 cents per pound

Now use your scratch paper to draw a blank option model like the one in Figure 3-7.

Now that you have your blank model, put in the purchase price as a horizontal line. From the put option's strike price draw a line toward the right horizontal at zero. This is the value of the option at expiration if the market is above the strike price. Now from the strike price on the futures price axis draw a line to where there is 400 intrinsic value. If you follow that line vertically down to the futures (horizontal) axis, you'll see what futures price you need to have 4.00 in premium. Now continue the line at the same angle across the graphic to the left and you will see how the potential gain is unlimited (excepting that the market cannot fall below zero). Your expiration line should end up above 600 in premium.

Your model should end up looking something like Figure 3-8.

What if we were hypothetically purchasing the 4000 lean hog call at 2.05 (2.05 × $400 = $820), what would the option model look like? Draw another blank model like Figure 3-7 and try to draw the expiration line. The premium should be the same although the breakeven vertical line should move slightly. Compare your work to Figure 3-9.

Since this is a call option, we are now looking for a positive change in the underlying futures price. It is a 4000 lean hog call, so the crossing point and vertical breakeven line should have moved to the opposite side of the 4200 futures price and your premium at expiration line should move upward to the right.

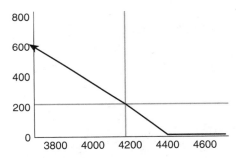

FIGURE 3-8
Hog option model

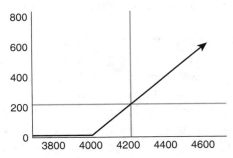

FIGURE 3-9
Hog call model

One of the great tools you will learn is the option model. Learning to graph your potential option trades will help you understand the potential for profit and loss as well as what might be time value risk and when it might occur.

TEST YOUR KNOWLEDGE 3-1

1. Put options are the right, but not the obligation, to be short the call option. True or False?
2. In a 50,000 lb feeder cattle contract a 1.00 call would cost $500. True or False?
3. A 500 soybean put would have a premium value of 12 at expiration if the market was at 512. True or False?
4. A purchased call option has _____ risk.
5. A 7300 lean hog put would have a breakeven of _____ if the option was purchased at 1.05.

BREAKEVEN ON PURCHASED OPTIONS

When purchasing options you must understand calculating the breakeven points when analyzing profit and loss, actual and potential. First let's look at purchased options prior to expiration. Prior to expiration we focus exclusively on the option premium rather than the underlying futures price. Let's look at an example in Figure 3-10.

We are once again purchasing the Dec corn 230 call for 12 ¾. Finding the breakeven on this option prior to expiration requires adding the costs of trading to the premium. Many option traders neglect this step of calculating breakeven which leads to misunderstandings of profit and loss.

We are purchasing the option for 12 ¾. Now let's add commissions and fees. To simplify things, let's say your commissions are $45 per round turn (*Round turn* means a full trade in and out), and the remainder of trading fees, such as exchange, brokerage, and National Futures Association add up to another $5 per round. Total of $50 per round turn. This one is simple because we know

Symbol	Str	OISet	ImpVol	Delta	DTE	ExpDate
CCCZ02200	200	30'0	0.2315	0.7858	171	11/23/02
CCCZ02210	210	23'2	0.2346	0.6919	171	11/23/02
CCCZ02220	220	17'2	0.2316	0.5896	171	11/23/02
CCCZ02230	230	12'6	0.2357	0.4832	171	11/23/02
CCCZ02240	240	9'5	0.2458	0.3889	171	11/23/02
CCCZ02250	250	7'1	0.2524	0.3074	171	11/23/02
CCCZ02260	260	5'3	0.2611	0.2426	171	11/23/02
CCCZ02270	270	4'1	0.2706	0.1922	171	11/23/02
CCCZ02280	280	3'1	0.2777	0.1508	171	11/23/02
CCCZ02290	290	2'3	0.2843	0.1183	171	11/23/02

FIGURE 3-10
December corn calls

that $50 equals 1 cent per bushel (5000 × 0.01 = $50). Now, we need to add cost of trading to the premium and find the breakeven.

$$12 \tfrac{3}{4} + 1 = 13 \tfrac{3}{4}$$

In other words, if we are to sell this option ahead of expiration, we must achieve a sale of at least 13 ¾ to breakeven on the sale of the option. Anything above 13 ¾ would be considered profit.

Option Expiration

When option's reach the expiration date, there are a few things that happen. First, it is determined if the option is in the money or out of the money. If the option is out of the money, it is removed from your account with no value. The entire premium is lost plus cost of trading as in the above example.

If the option is in the money, you have the choice to exercise the option into the underlying futures contract. Typically, this is done automatically by most clearing operations these days, but you want to check with your broker. If it is not done automatically, you want to communicate to your broker that you wish to exercise your option into the underlying futures. If the futures market was at 240 on expiration day, your option would be exercised into the futures at the 230 mark. In this case the clearing firm removes the 230 call and places a long futures position in your account at 230. Once the futures position is placed in your account, the limited risk aspect of a purchased call option is now ended and you have unlimited risk on the futures position.

Exercised Option Breakeven

Now we have an exercised option situation where the Dec 230 call is exercised into a long Dec corn futures position at 230. If we purchased a Dec corn 230 call for 12 ¾ and we added the cost of trading, this would make a total premium breakeven of 13 ¾. So to calculate breakeven in this situation now that the option is exercised, we must add that premium to the futures purchase price.

$$230 + 13 \, ¾ = 243 \, ¾$$

Remember, this scenario is on the option premium. The limited risk of the option ends once it is exercised into a futures position. In our option model, Figure 3-11, you can see. The option value line on the model starts with the premium (vertical axis) at 0 or in other words the option expiring worthless and begins to climb as the futures price (horizontal axis) reaches the strike price of 230. The option value line reaches the premium paid at 243 ¾. Remember, this line on our models is at option expiration and assumes no time value in the option.

Breakeven for Put Options

Calculating breakeven on purchased put options works exactly the same, with the only difference being that the put is the right to be short the underlying futures contract.

Let's try one and see if you can figure the breakeven on the option premium and the exercised futures price. We'll use the scenario in Figure 3-12.

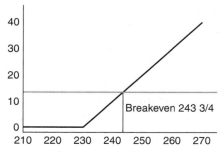

FIGURE 3-11
December corn option model

Symbol	Str	OISet	ImpVol	Delta	DTE	ExpDate
PCCZ02190	190	1'7	0.2229	0.1054	171	11/23/02
PCCZ02200	200	3'5	0.2225	0.1789	171	11/23/02
PCCZ02210	210	6'6	0.2305	0.2780	171	11/23/02
PCCZ02220	220	10'6	0.2327	0.3829	171	11/23/02
PCCZ02230	230	16'2	0.2413	0.4875	171	11/23/02
PCCZ02240	240	22'4	0.2456	0.5835	171	11/23/02
PCCZ02250	250	30'1	0.2597	0.6585	171	11/23/02

FIGURE 3-12
December corn puts

In Figure 3-12 we show the purchase of the Dec corn 230 put at 10 ¾. Calculate the option premium breakeven first. Use the same cost scenario as presented earlier for commissions and fees.

$$\text{Total premium } 10\,\tfrac{3}{4} + 1 = 11\,\tfrac{3}{4}$$

$$\text{Option breakeven } 220 - 11\,\tfrac{1}{4} = 208\,\tfrac{1}{4}$$

$$5000 \text{ bu} \times 0.1075 = \$537.50$$

$$\text{Add trading costs } (\$50 + \$537.50) = \$587.50$$

Remember that the put option is the right to be short the underlying futures. So, for the market to be going in the direction of the option, the futures price would have to be below the strike price.

Let's do one more to make sure you understand. We'll be using a more recent market and a different option chain, as shown in Figure 3-13. Figure 3-13 shows an option chain with both puts and calls listed. First let's detail the cocoa market. The contract is 10 metric tons and the underlying futures and options are in dollars per ton. So if the futures market is at 1450, then it is $1450 per metric ton.

Run a breakeven if we were to purchase the March 150 call option (15.00 call). The premium shown is 83. This makes the premium value in dollars $830.

$$\$83/\text{ton} \times 10 \text{ tons} = \$830$$

Now calculate the breakeven with a $50 total cost of trading.

$$\$830 + \$50 = \$870/10 \text{ (to get the point value) } 87$$

$$1500 + 87 = 1587$$

Contract	Open	High	Low	Last
CO-H05,C140		148	148	148
CO-H05,C145		113	113	113
CO-H05,C150		83	83	83
CO-H05,C155		58	58	58
CO-H05,C160	43	45	43	45
CO-H05,C165		29	29	29
CO-H05,C170	18	24	17	17
CO-H05,C175		13	13	13
CO-H05,P125		3	3	3
CO-H05,P130		6	6	6
CO-H05,P135		12	12	12
CO-H05,P140	12	22	12	12
CO-H05,P145		36	36	36
CO-H05,P150		56	56	56
CO-H05,P155	71	82	71	75
CO-H05,P160	95	117	95	95

FIGURE 3-13
March cocoa

TEST YOUR KNOWLEDGE 3-2

1. When calculating option breakeven, commissions and fees should be left out of the equation. True or False?
2. If my calculated option breakeven on a 500 soybean put is 23 ¾ then the market has to be at 523 ¾ for breakeven at expiration. True or False?
3. You should calculate breakevens only on grain options. True or False?
4. If (2) 6200 March feeder cattle calls (50,000 lbs) are purchased at 150, the futures breakeven is _____

Exercise 3-1   Try the breakeven on your own now buying the March Cocoa 145 put option. The answers are at the end of the chapter. Finding option breakeven is very important to understanding your profit and loss scenario. We recommend calculating the breakevens and creating a model for each position you consider.

Symbol	Str	OISet	ImpVol	Delta	DTE	ExpDate
CCCZ02200	200	30'0	0.2315	0.7858	171	11/23/02
CCCZ02210	210	23'2	0.2346	0.6919	171	11/23/02
CCCZ02220	220	17'2	0.2316	0.5896	171	11/23/02
CCCZ02230	230	12'6	0.2357	0.4832	171	11/23/02
CCCZ02240	240	9'5	0.2458	0.3889	171	11/23/02
CCCZ02250	250	7'1	0.2524	0.3074	171	11/23/02
CCCZ02260	260	5'3	0.2611	0.2426	171	11/23/02
CCCZ02270	270	4'1	0.2706	0.1922	171	11/23/02
CCCZ02280	280	3'1	0.2777	0.1508	171	11/23/02
CCCZ02290	290	2'3	0.2843	0.1183	171	11/23/02

FIGURE 3-14
December corn calls

LIQUIDATING OPTIONS

Before getting to selling options, we must talk about liquidating purchased options. As we have discussed, it is possible to liquidate and option position prior to the expiration of an option.

This is commonly referred to as selling an option; however, it is properly called *an offset*. When you want to liquidate a purchased option position, you have to reverse the buying process. Instead of bidding for the option you will place an offer to sell the same calendar month and strike price option that you currently own. Let's look at the example of the December 2002 corn calls again in Figure 3-14.

In Figure 3-14 we show the Dec corn 230 call highlighted. Let's say that hypothetically you had purchased this option at 6 and wanted to take the profit on the option at the price 12 ¾ shown in Figure 3-14. You would need to place an offer with your broker to offset the position by selling one Dec corn 230 call at 12 ¾. If someone sees your offer and chooses to pay the offer price, your option would be offset at the offer price. In this example that would be a profit of 6 ¾ minus cost of trading (12 ¾ sell price – 6 buy price = 6 ¾).

Let's look at the December corn put example again in Figure 3-15.

Figure 3-15 shows the Dec corn 220 put at a premium of 10 ¾. Let's say you purchased this option at a premium of 20 and you want to liquidate the option at the price shown. You would place an offer to sell the Dec 220 put at a premium

Symbol	Str	OISet	ImpVol	Delta	DTE	ExpDate
PCCZ02190	190	1'7	0.2229	0.1054	171	11/23/02
PCCZ02200	200	3'5	0.2225	0.1789	171	11/23/02
PCCZ02210	210	6'6	0.2305	0.2780	171	11/23/02
PCCZ02220	220	10'6	0.2327	0.3829	171	11/23/02
PCCZ02230	230	16'2	0.2413	0.4875	171	11/23/02
PCCZ02240	240	22'4	0.2456	0.5835	171	11/23/02
PCCZ02250	250	30'1	0.2597	0.6585	171	11/23/02

FIGURE 3-15
December corn puts

of 10 ¾. If someone sees your offer and chooses to buy at that price, then the trade would be made and the offset completed in your account.

When trading purchased options, liquidating ahead of expiration is often how you will realize profit on an option position or control a loss of premium. However, you should be focused on the expiration values and breakeven in the worst-case scenario when entering any purchased option position.

USING PROPER ORDER TERMINOLOGY

One of the most beneficial lessons to be learned in option or futures trading is to utilize proper terminology, so that there are no misunderstandings or miscommunications with your broker or order taker. As a broker, it's common to have customers incorrectly state their order as to buy and sell. Here are some recommendations for communicating with your broker for action on a purchased option. This is especially important for those who might use discount or online brokerage methods where a double check of your current position will not likely be done. When you want to acquire a new option position, there are a couple of common terms which your broker will recognize:

Buy This is the common term for acquiring a new option position.

Long This is also a very common term that your broker will not have any confusion with. (Go long is to buy.)

Sell For purchased options this term is used to liquidate a previously purchased option position.

To open This is the term for acquiring a new option position.

To close This is the term typically used to notify the order taker that you are liquidating an already existing option position.

Day order This term is to notify the broker or order taker that the order will be for the duration of today's session only.

GTC This acronym refers to good till canceled. This means that the order will remain active until it is filled, canceled, or the contract expires. This is also referred to as an *open order*. This order type is not available on certain markets.

Now let's talk about proper order format. You want to make sure you clarify all the points of the order and have it repeated back to you from the broker or order taker.

Make sure you state clearly the action (buy, sell), the quantity (1, 2) whatever, the contract month (i.e., March), the commodity (i.e., E-Mini S&P 500), the strike price (i.e., 900), the option type (i.e., call, put), the premium (i.e., 1.25), account action (i.e., open, close position), the order duration (i.e., day order, GTC order).

Buy 1 March E-mini S&P 500—900 call at 1.25 to open for the day.

If you are liquidating the option position on an open order, you would use the following format:

Sell 1 March E-mini S&P 500—900 call at 1.25 to close GTC.

The same format is used for purchased put options. Many traders become confused with the fact that put options are the right to short the market using a buy or a sell. Remember this is for purchased options.

Buy 1 March E-mini S&P 500—900 put at 1.25 to open for the day.

SELLING OPTIONS

The next step in your option education is learning about selling options. First let's talk a little about how you sell something you don't already own. As we mentioned in earlier discussions, futures contract trading is a two-party system where one party is offering the commodity and another is bidding for it. Options work exactly the same; someone is offering the right, someone else is bidding for it. With that in mind, option selling comes down to being the offering party. So, in essence you can think about option selling as creating the contract availability. When you make the offer, it makes the contract available for purchase.

Being the seller of the option sharply contrasts from being an option buyer. Let's outline the differences and keep in mind that for now we are just talking about individual options and not spreads or covered positions, which are discussed later in the book.

First let's go back to the beginning and look at the definition of an option and note the relationship for selling options: An option is a right, but not an obligation, to the underlying futures contract at a specified price and specified point in time.

When you are selling options you are offering this right to the purchaser. So as the seller you are providing the purchaser the right to the underlying futures at a specified price and at a specified point in time. We often refer to selling an option which is not previously owned as a *short option*.

As the seller of the option, you have the obligation to take the opposing position of the underlying futures from the buyer of the option should the option be exercised. For this obligation, the option seller receives the premium paid for the option, minus the costs of trading. Let's look at some of the advantages and disadvantages of being a seller of the option.

Disadvantages

Unlimited Risk   A short option carries unlimited risk potential. This is especially true for short call options because technically speaking a commodity price could go to about anything. Nothing says that crude oil couldn't go to $100/bbl or $1,000/bbl or $10,000/bbl. Yes it's not likely, but there is nothing stopping it. Short put options vary from this only in the fact that there is no futures price below zero. Yes, it's not financially feasible for most people to trade that way, but it's essentially true. Crude oil may be able to go to $1,000,000,000 per barrel, but it cannot fall below zero. Again, it's not usual for someone to be capable of risking tens of thousands of dollars per contract to zero, but if so, that's where the risk stops on short put positions.

Limited Gain   Option sellers receive only the premium from offering the option to the buyer. There is no other opportunity for monetary gain.

Margin   In contrast to buying options where the only margin required is that of the purchase price of the option, short options have margin requirement similar to that of the underlying futures contract. Usually it is a percentage of the margin for the full futures contract. This margin requirement can also increase or decrease depending on the distance from the current futures prices, or more specifically on the delta of the option. The higher the delta, the more margin required.

Expiration Risk   In the last section we discussed scenarios where purchased options expire and are exercised into the underlying futures contract. As the option seller you are obligated to accept the opposite side of the underlying futures position. This risk also exists anytime prior to expiration. The option purchaser has the right to exercise the option at any time prior to expiration as well as at expiration. This is not common because there is typically time value in an option prior to expiration. Occasionally, deep in-the-money options may have lost all time value and may be exercised by the purchaser into the underlying futures. This usually occurs when there is low liquidity in the option being offset.

Liquidity   The risk associated with liquidity runs on both sides of the trading process. Option buyers and sellers can at times be at risk to the availability of an offsetting contract reasonably bid or offered at the time when you are trying to liquidate. With short option positions you can offset prior to expiration by offering to buy the option back. In other terms, you pay the premium for the right to be long the option and this can be at a profit or loss, but can be dictated at times by the availability of the offsetting position. This is not a normal circumstance, but you should be aware of this risk.

Traders new to selling options often ask why take this kind of risk for a limited gain? The simple answer is the disadvantages of buying options are often the advantages of selling options.

Advantages

Time Decay   What makes buying options risky is what makes option sellers money. As time moves forward, the option seller has more of the premium from the option sale. The buyers depreciating asset is now your appreciating asset.

Volatility   Options which have higher than average implied volatility tend to have inflated premium which may reduce when volatility changes for the futures market. Meaning that this premium is captured for the seller.

Odds   This is a subjective area to an extent, but it is commonly stated that 80 to 90% of purchased options expire worthless. Statistically it's 50-50, but because many traders choose to purchase deep out-of-the-money options they experience a higher rate of loss.

As the option seller you share similar market risks as the option buyer. As with any investment, liquidity can always be an issue. Abnormal market conditions may affect the ability of both an option purchaser and seller to liquidate open market positions.

TEST YOUR KNOWLEDGE 3-3

1. The option seller is bidding for option positions. True or False?
2. A sold option position is often referred to as a short option. True or False?
3. A short option has unlimited profit potential. True or False?
4. Level of volume and open interest is _____.
5. The deposit or performance bond required for trading is _____.

SELLING CALL OPTIONS

Now that we have talked a little about selling options in general. Let's talk about specific option strategy. First we'll start with selling call options and look at how the definition of an option relates.

We know that a call option is the right but not the obligation to be long the underlying futures at a specific price and point time, so as the seller of the call option *you provide the right to the buyer and therefore you do have the obligation.* Let's look at a new example in Figure 3-16. We have changed the table to show a little more information about the option. First you can see a new bar at the top showing the underlying future, price, volatility expiration, and underlying interest rate (delta). This is a Dec coffee future and call options.

Here are some details about the market shown in Figure 3-16: The coffee contract represented is NYBOT Coffee and is 37,500 lbs per contract. The price is in dollars per 100 lbs. So the multiplier per point is $375 per full point. You can multiply it two ways

Contract weight × price ÷ by 100 (37,500 × 2.03/100 = $761.25)

Or

$$\$375 \times 2.03 = \$761.25$$

In this example we are going to sell outright the Dec coffee 85 call option for a premium of 2.03. As the seller, you receive the premium ($761.25). Let's first look at how we achieve this premium. Selling this call option means that a buyer has paid $761.25 for the option position. These funds are placed in your account. Now let's look at the risk and reward of this position. The option is an 85 call

KCZ3	65.35	0.1500 11/14/03	107 5.00%
Option	Price	Imp. Vol.	Delta
Dec 65.00C	6.00	0.4209	0.5466
Dec 67.50C	5.12	0.4340	0.4847
Dec 70.00C	4.40	0.4479	0.4292
Dec 72.50C	3.80	0.4614	0.3800
Dec 75.00C	3.30	0.4746	0.3369
Dec 77.50C	2.89	0.4882	0.2996
Dec 80.00C	2.55	0.5018	0.2674
Dec 82.50C	2.27	0.5156	0.2399
Dec 85.00C	2.03	0.5289	0.2160

FIGURE 3-16
December coffee

option so at expiration if the underlying futures price is above 85, the option would be in the money and at risk to be exercised into the underlying futures contract at the strike price of 85. If the market was below the 85 mark, the option would expire and as the seller you would receive the entire premium; but don't forget to subtract your costs of trading.

Let's say that the Dec coffee market is at 87.50 at expiration. The option would be in the money and the contract exercised into a futures position.

In this example you are exercised into a short futures position. A call is the right but not the obligation to be long the market, so as the seller of this right you are obligated on a short call to take the short side of the market when exercised. Remember it's the opposite of the right given the option buyer.

For simplicity, let's assume that the underlying contract is offset at this same price. The futures position is entered at 85.00 (the strike price) and is exited upon expiration at 87.50.

$$8500 - 87.50 = 2.50 \text{ loss on offset of the exercised call option}$$

$$2.50 \times \$375 = \$937.50$$

In addition to the loss here, you must add to the totals the costs of trading, including the costs of the option being exercised into the underlying futures. You have costs and fees charged when you enter the position, when you are exercised into the underlying futures, and when you offset the underlying futures. To make things simple let's say the three charges total $50 (although it would likely be more with many brokers). This takes our total loss to $987.50.

Now we have to remember the premium we received when the option was sold, which was $761.25, and subtract that from the loss to figure the net of the position.

$$\$987.50 - \$761.25 = \$236.25$$

Let's try another example from Figure 3-16.

For this example we'll use 85 call again and assume the market is at 86.10 at expiration. Get your scratch paper and calculate the profit or loss on this example.

$$\text{Gross loss} = 85.00 - 86.10 = (1.10)$$

$$(1.10) \times \$375 = (\$412.50)$$

$$\text{Net} = (412.50) + \$761.25 = \$348.75$$

In this example, the position turned a profit rather than a loss despite the market's expiring in the money. Remember to subtract your cost of trading from your profits or add it to your losses.

As we mentioned earlier, you can also purchase back the option at a point prior to expiration. This often is done as profit taking or risk reduction once the option has lost the majority of its time value or as a risk-management tactic to stop losses, similar to a stop in futures trading.

Using the example above again, let's say we sell the option for 2.03 as in our other examples and 60 days from now the option has lost some time value or the market has moved even farther away from the 85.00 strike price. The option's value is now 1.00 and you want to take this profit and take no further risk on the option. You place a bid on the market to purchase the 85.00 call option at 1.00 and it is filled. You now have the long right and the short obligation in the same account so the options automatically offset each other leaving you with the cash difference between the buy and the sell.

In this example if we purchased the option at 1.00 and sold it at 2.03, you would have a gross profit from the position of 1.03 minus the costs of trading.

$$1.03 \times \$375 = \$386.25 \text{ minus cost of trading}$$

So even though the option expired in the money by a slight amount the option position was still profitable. Always remember to factor in the premium captured when calculating your total profit or loss.

Later in this chapter we'll discuss taking profit on short options prior to expiration.

TEST YOUR KNOWLEDGE 3-4

1. When you sell a call option you have the right to be short the underlying futures position. True or False?

2. If you are short the 82 call option and the underlying futures market is at 81.90 at option expiration, your option would be in the money. True or False?

3. You always lose money when the short option expires in the money and is exercised into the underlying futures position. True or False?

4. The risk of selling a call option is _____.

5. Always subtract your _____ costs from captured premium.

SELLING PUT OPTIONS

We know that a put option is the right, but not the obligation, to be short the underlying futures at a specific price and point time, so as the seller of the put option you provide the right to the buyer, and therefore you do have the obligation just as it was with selling calls in our previous section. Let's look at a new example in Figure 3-17.

KCZ3	65.35	0.1500 11/14/03	107 5.00%	
Option	**Price**	**Imp. Vol.**	**Delta**	
Dec 50.00P	0.35	0.3777	−0.0561	
Dec 52.50P	0.62	0.3798	−0.0902	
Dec 55.00P	1.02	0.3818	−0.1345	
Dec 57.50P	1.57	0.3833	−0.1882	
Dec 60.00P	2.30	0.3855	−0.2501	
Dec 62.50P	3.35	0.3983	−0.3198	
Dec 65.00P	4.61	0.4112	−0.3887	
Dec 67.50P	6.10	0.4270	−0.4536	
Dec 70.00P	7.75	0.4423	−0.5126	

FIGURE 3-17
December coffee

To keep it simple, we'll use coffee again, only this time our example is the Dec 55 coffee put option. Remember it is $375 per full point.

With the sale of the Dec 55 put, we capture premium in the amount of $382.50. The Dec 55 put option is how far out of the money?

Calculating the risk and reward of this position is the same as for the call discussion only switched for the put option. If the underlying futures price at option expiration is above the 55.00 mark, the option would expire worthless and the seller would capture the entire premium of $382.50 minus costs and fees of trading. If the underlying futures market was below the 55.00 mark at option expiration, we then would have to calculate to see our profit and loss (P&L). Let's do an example.

The Dec coffee futures are at 52.98 at option expiration and because this position would be in the money, we are exercised into the underlying futures. Now because this is a put option we are obligated to take the long side of the futures market from 55.00. Our calculated P&L is

$$52.98 - 55.00 = 2.02, \text{ or } \$757.50 \text{ loss}$$

We captured premium of $382.50 so we can subtract that from the loss

$$2.02 - 1.02 = 1.00, \text{ or } \$375 \text{ loss}$$

Don't forget to factor in the costs and fees of trading and add them to any loss you might have or subtract them from any gain.

Let's put together an example, from Figure 3-17 for you to do on your own and let's see if you can figure the P&L.

Exercise 3-2 Using Figure 3-17 calculate the P&L for selling 2 of the 62.50 puts if the market was at the current futures price at expiration.

CALCULATING BREAKEVEN FOR SHORT OPTIONS

As we did with purchased options, we need to know before we enter a trade where the breakeven for options selling is. The calculation for breakeven for short options is similar to the process for purchased options, but we just want to make sure the concept is clear.

Short Call Options The risk on this option is to be short the underlying futures if exercised at the strike price, so we need to apply the premium to that price to get our breakeven. In Figure 3-18, the 96 call option is priced at 0.0184,

HUV3	0.8895	0.1500	9/25/03	53	5.00%
Option	**Price**	**Imp. Vol.**	**Delta**		
Oct 0.8900C	0.0420	0.3148	0.5183		
Oct 0.9000C	0.0376	0.3157	0.4816		
Oct 0.9100C	0.0336	0.3170	0.4457		
Oct 0.9200C	0.0299	0.3178	0.4108		
Oct 0.9300C	0.0266	0.3192	0.3774		
Oct 0.9400C	0.0236	0.3206	0.3454		
Oct 0.9500C	0.0209	0.3220	0.3151		
Oct 0.9600C	0.0184	0.3228	0.2861		
Oct 0.9700C	0.0162	0.3240	0.2592		
Oct 0.9800C	0.0142	0.3248	0.2338		
Oct 0.9900C	-----	-----	0.2054		
Oct 0.7900P	0.0084	0.3137	−0.1453		
Oct 0.8000P	0.0103	0.3139	−0.1707		
Oct 0.8100P	0.0125	0.3141	−0.1985		
Oct 0.8200P	-----	-----	−0.2388		
Oct 0.8300P	0.0178	0.3140	−0.2597		
Oct 0.8400P	0.0210	0.3142	−0.2931		
Oct 0.8500P	0.0246	0.3147	−0.3280		
Oct 0.8600P	0.0478	0.4652	−0.3873		
Oct 0.8700P	0.0328	0.3148	−0.4004		
Oct 0.8800P	-----	-----	−0.4380		
Oct 0.8900P	-----	-----	−0.4730		

FIGURE 3-18
October unleaded

unleaded gasoline is a 42,000 gallon contract, making each 0.01 worth $420. To determine breakeven add the premium to the futures price:

$$0.8895 + 0.0184 = 0.0979$$

Short Put Options   Here the risk is opposite, being long the underlying futures, so we have to create the opposite mathematics. Let's look at the 84 put option using Figure 3-18.

$$0.8895 - 0.0210 = 0.8685 \text{ (futures price)}$$

With these calculations, you know where the underlying futures must be at option expiration for your trade to be profitable. Don't forget to factor in the costs of trading.

TEST YOUR KNOWLEDGE 3-5

1. When you sell a put option you have the right to be short the underlying futures position. True or False?

2. If you are short the 62 put option and the underlying futures market is at 62.20 at option expiration, your option would be in the money. True or False?

3. You should determine breakeven on short option positions to determine where your risk begins on an exercised underlying futures position. True or False?

4. If you sell a 6800 lean hog put for 0.95, your futures breakeven is _____.

5. Selling a December 6800 lean hog put for 0.95 captures _____ dollars in premium (40,000 lb contract).

OFFSETTING PRIOR TO EXPIRATION

So far in selling options we have discussed option sales which eventually are exercised into the underlying futures and how to calculate P&L and breakeven. An advantage to selling option premium is that there is the opportunity to exit the option position prior to expiration for either risk management or profit taking. When you have purchased an option position, you have the opportunity to liquidate that option position by offering your option to the market at the price you would like to get for it or at the price you see on the market currently.

The process is the same for option sellers in that you are reversing your position. Since you are short the option, you would bid to buy the option back at a price of your choice or at the current market price. Let's look at the NYMEX unleaded gasoline example in Figure 3-18. Remember that unleaded gasoline is a 42,000 gallon contract. Each point is $420.

Let's look at the example of the 9700 call option, selling the option at the price of 0.0162. If the underlying futures market were to fall away from the strike price or the option were to lose time value, the option premium would be less over time. Hypothetically, let's say the option premium value falls to 0.0062. If you were to successfully bid for the purchase of the option at 0.0062 it would offset the short option position in your account. The P&L would look like this:

Original selling price − repurchase price = P&L

0.0162 − 0.0062 = 0.0100 ($420)

The put option P&L looks very similar; subtract the repurchase premium from the original purchase price.

Remember, when trying to repurchase a short option position that you must make a bid on the exact option month and strike price in order to offset the position.

OFFSETTING TO CONTROL RISK

One reason to offset a short option position prior to expiration is as a part of your risk-management strategy. Different schools of thought exist as to how to manage naked short option risk, so we'll outline some basic risk-management strategies. First you should know that you can utilize many of the functions of futures orders when buying and selling options.

Option contracts can usually be purchased or sold on limit orders. Most systems are now allowing stop orders as well. This is a significant advantage to risk management, because you can offset short options with prepositioned orders. To purchase an existing short option to control risk you are using the same process as we discussed for profit taking. You are bidding for the same option strike price and contract month as the one you sold, only with a price that may involve a loss. Let's go through a couple of strategies.

Technical chart management, as a rule, is our first line of defense. If you are an experienced technical futures trader, you might utilize your futures risk-management strategy as the point to indicate the exit on any short option position that might be going against you. In short, with option trading you are working typically with out-of-the-money options that are going to have a delta lower than 1.00 of the underlying futures. This often allows the technical trader to be a bit more liberal with the support and resistance, but we generally try to follow some basic market rules like high/low resistance and support, moving averages, and trading range analysis. If you use more advanced technical methods, those can certainly be applied, and if you are not able to watch the market, your broker may do it for you.

Stops Based on Premium   We use as a general rule some sort of open stop based on the option premium versus the original sale premium. This can be double the original premium, triple, or whatever makes sense financially for you, but you should have this last line of defense as an open order in markets that allow it.

Repurchase Low Premium   At times we will recommend to repurchase option premium which has fallen to very low levels prior to expiration. Often this happens if the underlying futures move away from the strike price after the option is sold and the premium falls to near worthless. The idea here is that markets cycle. A market that has fallen is likely to be bought and a market that has risen is likely to be sold. So if you have a successful short option trade which has some time prior to expiration and is inexpensive (comparatively) to the original sale, buying back the option is a method of controlling future risk. There is no worse feeling than having a successful short option position come back and be stopped out because of market cycles. Don't be afraid to take profits, as the old saying goes, you'll never go broke taking profits.

KEY TERMS

Day order   An order placed with your trader or broker that is to be good for the current day's trade only.

GTC/open order   This order is good till canceled; in other words, the order remains open each day until it is canceled or the contract expires.

Long   This the common terminology for buying the market, anticipating the market to rise.

Margin   Funds placed in reserve as a performance bond against risk-oriented trades in your account.

Offset/liquidation   Closing out existing positions in your account by placing the exact opposite position in your account.

Option breakeven   The futures price at which the option premium and trading costs are recovered at option expiration.

Option exercise   The process of converting an option into the underlying futures at the strike price of the option.

Short   This is the common terminology for selling the market, anticipating the market to fall.

To close   Using this term notifies the trader or broker that your position order is to close out an existing position.

To open   This is the term for initiating a new order in your account.

CHAPTER TEST

1. Which of the following is NOT an advantage of purchasing options?
   (a) Limited risk
   (b) Unlimited profit potential
   (c) Multiple option positions
   (d) Time decay

2. Liquidity is a risk to buying and selling options because
   (a) Futures sometimes expire before options.
   (b) Brokers put in option trades after futures trades.
   (c) Bids and offers on option premium can be far apart.
   (d) Options expire when there is no trading in the option.

3. CBOT corn is 5000 bushels per contract. If the 230 call is 0.14 what is the amount in dollars?
   (a) $70,000
   (b) $7,000
   (c) $700
   (d) $1,400

4. If you purchase the 230 call at 0.14, where do the underlying futures have to be at expiration to break even assuming your trading costs are $50?
   (a) 215
   (b) 230
   (c) 244
   (d) 245

5. Which of the following has all of the necessary information to properly communicate an order to your broker?
   (a) Sell 1 March E-mini S&P 500—900 call at 1.25 to close GTC.
   (b) Buy 10 January Feeder Cattle 8200 puts at .95 to open, for the day.
   (c) Both a and b
   (d) Neither

6. When a short option expires in the money you are obligated to
   (a) Accept the underlying futures position.
   (b) Liquidate your position immediately.

(c) Settle with the buyer in cash.

(d) None of the above.

7. If you sell the Dec unleaded gasoline (42,000 gal) 0.9400 call for 0.0200 and if the option expires and the underlying futures are offset at 9700, your loss is what in dollars (assume trading costs of $50)?

(a) $420

(b) $470

(c) $240

(d) What loss?

8. Which of the following is NOT an advantage of selling option premium?

(a) High implied volatility

(b) Time value decay

(c) Limited risk

(d) Statistical odds

9. When selling options which of the following is NOT good risk-management practice?

(a) Follow your broker's hunch.

(b) Repurchase decayed option premium.

(c) Premium value based safety stop.

(d) Technical futures market analysis.

10. Which of the following terms represents options which may be overvalued?

(a) Elevated theta

(b) Elevated gamma

(c) Elevated implied volatility

ANSWERS TO TESTS

Test Your Knowledge 3-1

1. False. A put option is the right but not the obligation to be short the underlying futures. 2. True. 50,000 lb × 0.0100 = $500; remember cattle is quoted

cents per hundred. 3. False. The premium value at 512 would be zero; it would expire worthless. The futures would have to be 488 to have a premium value of 12 at expiration. 4. Limited Risk. 5. 71.95 (7300 − 1.05 = 71.95).

Test Your Knowledge 3-2

1. False. Not adding commission and fees is one of the biggest mistakes traders make. 2. False. This is a put option; the breakeven would be 523 ¾. If it were a call option, 476 ¼ would be the put breakeven. 3. False. You should calculate breakeven on every position you consider. 4. 63.50 (6200 + 150 = 6350).

Test Your Knowledge 3-3

1. False. The option seller is creating the offer side of the two-party system by making the contract available. 2. True. Short is the common term in the market for a sold option position. 3. False. A short option position has a limited gain potential. The gain is limited to the amount of the premium realized from the sale of the option to the purchaser. 4. Liquidity. 5. Margin.

Test Your Knowledge 3-4

1. False. Remember from our definition of an option that when you short a call option you have the obligation, not the right, to accept the underlying short futures position if exercised. 2. False. Just like with purchased options, the 82 call would be out of the money at any price below 82.00. 82.00 and above would be in the money. 3. False. As in our example above, the premium captured should be factored into the total P&L. 4. Unlimited (risk). 5. Trading (costs).

Test Your Knowledge 3-5

1. False. Remember from our definition of an option that when you short a put option you have the obligation, not the right, to accept the underlying long futures position if exercised. 2. False. Just like with purchased options, the 62

put would be out of the money at any price above 62.00. 62.00 and below would be in the money. 3. True. Calculating breakeven is an important part of risk management. 4. 67.05 (6800 − 95 = 6705). 5. $380 (40,000 × 0.0095).

Exercise 3-1

$36/ton × 10 tons = $360
$360 + $50 = $410/10 (to get the point value) 41
1450 − 41 = 1409 breakeven

Exercise 3-2

(3.35 × $375) × 2 = $2,512.50 minus costs of trading

Chapter Test

1. d. Time value decay is a significant disadvantage to buying options.
2. c. Bids and offers can be far apart on options, especially in markets with slow or thin trade.
3. c. 5000 bu. × 0.14 = $700.
4. d. 230 strike price + 14 premium + 1 trading fees = 245.
5. c. Both orders are correct.
6. a. When you are short the option, you do have the obligation to the underlying futures.
7. b. 4400 call + 200 premium = 4600; 4700 futures settlement − 4600 = 100 or $420 + trading costs = $470.
8. c. Short option positions have unlimited risk.
9. a. The hunch—make sure you have an analytical or monetary stop.
10. c. The elevated implied volatility would show demand and possible inflated pricing for the option.

CHAPTER 4

OPTION SPREAD STRATEGIES

In this chapter we discover a variety of spread strategies used with options. First we discuss the basic categories of option spreads, including their variations. Then we'll discuss advanced option strategy and technique.

- Vertical spreads
- Ratio spreads
- Delta spreads
- Advanced option spreads
- Spread technique and strategy

VERTICAL SPREADS

Our spread education starts with basic vertical spreads. First let's define what a vertical spread is and how it relates to our definition of an option. A *vertical spread* is the simultaneous purchase and sale of options at different strike prices and/or different contract months. This means that with a vertical spread you will be purchasing an option at one-strike price and selling an option at another strike price at the same time.

Let's relate this to our definition of an option: We now have the right, but not the obligation, to the underling futures at a specific price and at a specific point in time with the purchased option.

We also now have the obligation to accept the underlying futures at another specific price and/or point in time from the option sale.

The purchased option therefore creates an offset to the risk of the short option by providing the right to the futures at another strike price whether the spread is done as a debit (purchased option premium higher than the short option premium) or credit. We'll discuss credit spreads later in the chapter.

Bull Call Spreads

To understand vertical spreads better, we'll start with the bull call spread. The bull call spread utilizes the purchase of a call option at a lower strike price combined with the sale of a call at a higher strike price. This combination creates a spread of profit potential between the strike prices, and the risk of the short call option is offset by the purchased call option position. Let's look at the example in Figure 4-1.

We have highlighted the Dec crude 30.00 call purchased at 1.87 along with the sale of the Dec crude 33.00 call at 0.76. First let's look at the cost of the trade and then we'll model the profit and loss (P&L). Crude Oil is a 1000 barrel contract quoted in dollars per barrel. To calculate the cost of a bull call spread remember this formula:

$$\text{Purchase option premium} - \text{short option premium} = \text{total}$$

$$1.87 - 0.76 = 1.11$$

$$1000 \text{ barrels} \times 1.11 = \$1110$$

Don't forget to add your trading costs to the total premium.

We now have purchased the Dec 30.00 call option which gives us the right to the underlying futures long at 30.00. We have sold the 33.00 call, giving us the obligation to accept the underlying futures short at 33.00; however, because we have the right at 30, the risk of the short call at 33 is eliminated. To demonstrate this let's assume that the underlying futures market expires 34.00 and both options are exercised.

Thinking back to your purchased option discussions, remember that the 30 call when exercised gives us the underlying futures position long at 30.00. The 33 call would become a short futures position at 33.00. The resulting transaction would be

$$33.00 - 30.00 = 3.00$$

$$1000 \times 3.00 = \$3000$$

Calculate the P&L by subtracting your cost from the gross profit:

CLZ3	30.09	0.1500	11/17/03	91	5.00%

Option	Price	Imp. Vol.	Delta
Dec 28.50C	2.74	0.3214	0.6540
Dec 29.00C	2.44	0.3190	0.6145
Dec 29.50C	2.14	0.3132	0.5739
Dec 30.00C	1.87	0.3091	0.5318
Dec 30.50C	1.63	0.3066	0.4891
Dec 31.00C	1.42	0.3056	0.4470
Dec 31.50C	1.21	0.3011	0.4042
Dec 32.00C	1.04	0.3001	0.3640
Dec 32.50C	0.89	0.2994	0.3256
Dec 33.00C	0.76	0.2991	0.2898
Dec 33.50C	0.65	0.2997	0.2571
Dec 26.50P	0.61	0.3373	−0.1983
Dec 27.00P	0.72	0.3322	−0.2279
Dec 27.50P	0.85	0.3281	−0.2606
Dec 28.00P	1.00	0.3246	−0.2960
Dec 28.50P	1.16	0.3196	−0.3331
Dec 29.00P	1.35	0.3166	−0.3727
Dec 29.50P	1.55	0.3119	−0.4136
Dec 30.00P	1.78	0.3089	−0.4558
Dec 30.50P	2.04	0.3074	−0.4983
Dec 31.00P	2.32	0.3058	−0.5405

FIGURE 4-1
December crude oil

$$\$3000 - \$1100 = \$1900 \text{ profit (minus trading costs)}$$

When both options are exercised into the underlying futures position, the offset is automatic because your account has a long and short of the same contract.

Bull Call Spread Advantages

The bull call spread is the most basic of purchased or debit spreads and is the most commonly used option spread. The bull call spread has several advantages to outright purchasing the option premium.

The bull call spread combines the strategy of buying call option premium for limited risk with the advantage of selling option premium to reduce costs. Bull call spreads make it possible for option traders to purchase at-the-money or close-to-the-money premium because of the cost reduction.

While we are taking advantage of the short option premium captured from the call sale, we are not increasing the risk of the spread from the limited risk of the purchased option because the purchased option continuously covers the short call option premium (as long as the purchased option is at a higher delta than the short option premium).

The bull call spread has certain disadvantages as well. The spread is limited in risk, but it is also limited in profit potential because of the short call position.

The bull call spread is often considered "slow" because of the reduction in option delta. As you'll remember from earlier chapters, delta is the expression of percent change between the option and the underlying futures position. The bull call spread combines the long delta of the purchased call option with the short delta of the sold call option, which reduces the overall delta of the position. So, in other words, it has less movement with the underlying futures.

Let's look at how the delta is affected in the example in Figure 4-1.

The delta calculation is fairly simple; you just need to remember a couple quick facts. Long option delta is positive; short option delta is negative. You're always adding deltas, but don't forget that when adding negative delta you are adding a negative number. (You would subtract the delta.)

In the example in Figure 4-1, we have the CLZ 30.00 call showing a delta of 0.5318 and the 33 call showing a delta of 0.2898.

$$0.5318 - 0.2898 = 0.242 \text{ (round to 0.24, or 24\%)}$$

This bull call spread offers a delta of 24% of the underlying futures. For each dollar the futures move the spread will move a quarter. Remember though that as the market moves the deltas change, so keep track of the delta of your trade as time goes on.

Bull call spreads offer an advantage in long-term trading range situations. We find many situations where the bull call spread is effective, but ideally you might look for markets that may be moving higher seasonally or from a change in market fundamentals. The lower delta of the trade or "slow" movement makes the trade ideal for targeting trading ranges and allowing the trade to move closer to expiration.

Remember also that as the market moves toward expiration, your trade will suffer time value decay like any purchased option position; however, so will the short option, giving you some offset to the decaying premium.

Bear Put Spreads

The opposite side of the bull call spread we just completed is the bear put spread. This spread uses the same format as the bull call spread whereby were are purchasing an option at, in or nearer to the money than the option that is sold or shorted. These basic option combinations employ our first use of short option premium to apply toward our purchased option premium to reduce premium risk or financially allow the purchase of an option much closer to the current market.

To review, because we now have the right to be short the underlying futures price from our purchased option, we have no additional risk from taking the obligation to the underlying futures at a lower strike price. We then have a range of profit potential between the two strike prices as we did with the bull call spread only with our target being a lower underlying futures price over time.

Let's look at Figure 4-2, which is for the same commodity as in our example. Remember, look at a commodity specification sheet if you need help with values throughout this book. A current commodity specification sheet can be obtained from your broker or the futures exchanges and are available online. Crude oil again is a 1000 barrel contract quoted in dollars per barrel.

In our example, we show the calls in a darker gray to reduce confusion, and we have highlighted a buy and sell on the put side in a lighter gray. You will notice that in our example we are purchasing the Dec crude oil 30.00 put option at 1.78, and we are selling the Dec crude oil 27.50 put option at 0.85. Let's first look at the premium cost of this trade:

$$1.78 - 0.85 = 0.93$$

$$1000 \text{ barrels} \times 0.93 = \$930$$

Now let's take a look at the profit potential of this position if the underlying futures were to expire with both options in the money:

$$30.00 - 27.50 = 2.50$$

$$2.50 - 0.93 = 1.57$$

$$1000 \text{ barrels} \times 1.57 = \$1570$$

The maximum profit potential for this spread is $1570. We use this spread as an example, but typically in actual trading we recommend risk (premium cost) to reward (profit potential) ratios that are a bit higher. This one is a bit less than 2:1; we like to have bull call and bear put ratios exceed 2:1, ideally reaching 3:1

CLZ3	30.09	0.1500	11/17/03	91	5.00%

Option	Price	Imp. Vol.	Delta
Dec 28.50C	2.74	0.3214	0.6540
Dec 29.00C	2.44	0.3190	0.6145
Dec 29.50C	2.14	0.3132	0.5739
Dec 30.00C	1.87	0.3091	0.5318
Dec 30.50C	1.63	0.3066	0.4891
Dec 31.00C	1.42	0.3056	0.4470
Dec 31.50C	1.21	0.3011	0.4042
Dec 32.00C	1.04	0.3001	0.3640
Dec 32.50C	0.89	0.2994	0.3256
Dec 33.00C	0.76	0.2991	0.2898
Dec 33.50C	0.65	0.2997	0.2571
Dec 26.50P	0.61	0.3373	−0.1983
Dec 27.00P	0.72	0.3322	−0.2279
Dec 27.50P	0.85	0.3281	−0.2606
Dec 28.00P	1.00	0.3246	−0.2960
Dec 28.50P	1.16	0.3196	−0.3331
Dec 29.00P	1.35	0.3166	−0.3727
Dec 29.50P	1.55	0.3119	−0.4136
Dec 30.00P	1.78	0.3089	−0.4558
Dec 30.50P	2.04	0.3074	−0.4983
Dec 31.00P	2.32	0.3058	−0.5405

FIGURE 4-2
December crude oil puts

or 4:1. This means that the profit potential should be at least double the premium you pay for the spread.

Selling Prior to Expiration

As with individual options, vertical spreads have the advantage of being able to be removed prior to expiration or split up to take advantage of market position or potential.

To understand removing option spreads prior to expiration, we need to understand a bit more about how to place these orders with your broker or trading assistant. With individual options, we know that when purchasing option premium we are bidding for the option premium at a certain premium or we are using a market order to take the best offer available. With short option premium, we are offering the option at a certain price or we are using a market order to take the best bid available.

With vertical spreads like the bull call and bear put spreads, we are using both of these at the same time. Rather than putting in each side of the trade as an individual option, the exchanges allow for orders to be placed as a combined premium where both options must be traded at the same time and at the specified combined spread premium value. You may, of course, trade them as individual options if you wish when initiating or closing out the trade, but the spread order ensures proper premium pricing and that you will have both sides if the trade is executed.

To use this spread order technique to open your position, you need to calculate the combined premium for the option spread as we did in the examples. Once you calculate the current premium, you need to decide if this is the premium you wish to bid for the spread or if you prefer another amount. You then need to let your trader or broker know that you are placing a spread order and give the option strike prices to be bought and sold using the techniques we discussed in Chapter 3. Then give them the combined premium *bid* for the spread. With this information the option broker on the floor of the exchange will know to execute both options to achieve this premium value if possible.

When removing a spread prior to any expiration, we need to reverse this process. Just remember that the option you purchased will now be sold and the option you sold will now need to be purchased. Again calculate the current premium and decide if you wish to *offer* the spread for this premium or another amount. As before, give the trade information to your trading assistant or broker and the offer premium value for the spread. This way the spread will be removed as one trade. Don't forget, that even though you are placing these trades as a spread, you will still be charged trading fees and commissions on both option positions.

The strategy of removing trades prior to expiration can be considered risk management or profit taking. With either of these two spreads, as the market moves, the premium values change according to the delta and volatility of the option versus the underlying futures. In addition, time value decay is continuously working on the short option premium. If time and market price work in your favor, the spread may have a nice profit position sometime prior to expiration. Calculate the current spread premium frequently to see where you are and determine if removing the spread make sense. Then use the procedure above to offer your position at a profit.

Use the example in Figure 4-2 to answer the questions in Test Your Knowledge 4-1.

TEST YOUR KNOWLEDGE 4-1

1. The bear put spread buying the 30.50 put and selling the 28.00 would be 1.04. True or False?
2. The calculated delta of the example spread is 0.7154. True or False?
3. If you bought the 31 put and sold the 30 put, you would have a maximum profit potential of $1000. True or False?
4. Buying the 31.00 crude oil call for 147 and selling the 33.00 call for 76 would have a profit potential of _____.
5. Offsetting the spread from question 4 at 1.01 would yield a net profit of _____.

RISK REVERSAL SPREADS

The risk reversal spread is another commonly used spread in commodity and stock trading. This spread is often used in combination trading with futures or long stock positions and can be one of the most aggressive option market positions.

The risk reversal like other vertical spreads uses a long option or purchased option and a short option; the difference here is that we are combining options that both benefit from the movement of the underlying futures in the same direction. Options that would benefit from the market moving higher would be a short put and a long call. Both have a long delta and, when combined, create a long risk reversal. A short call and long put both benefit from the market moving down and, when combined, create a short risk reversal with a combined short delta.

Long risk reversals create the obligation to the underlying futures at a particular price and point in time, while the long call gives you the right, but not the obligation, at a particular price and point in time. The opposite is true for the short risk reversal.

Let's look at an example in Figure 4-3. The cocoa contract is 10 metric tons quoted in dollars per metric ton.

In Figure 4-3 we have highlighted a buy of the Jan cocoa 1700 call and a sell of the Jan cocoa 1400 put. We now need to calculate the premium involved. The

CCH4	1641	0.1500	12/5/03	86	5.00%

Option	Price	Imp. Vol.	Delta
Jan 1500C	200.00	0.3915	0.7065
Jan 1550C	168.00	0.3858	0.6471
Jan 1600C	141.00	0.3864	0.5835
Jan 1650C	116.00	0.3829	0.5192
Jan 1700C	95.00	0.3820	0.4557
Jan 1750C	78.00	0.3844	0.3961
Jan 1800C	63.00	0.3845	0.3397
Jan 1850C	50.00	0.3828	0.2870
Jan 1900C	40.00	0.3842	0.2414
Jan 1950C	32.00	0.3863	0.2019
Jan 2000C	25.00	0.3859	0.1659
Jan 1300P	15.00	0.3949	−0.0938
Jan 1350P	22.00	0.3912	−0.1292
Jan 1400P	32.00	0.3914	−0.1739
Jan 1450P	44.00	0.3881	−0.2236
Jan 1500P	60.00	0.3890	−0.2809
Jan 1550P	78.00	0.3856	−0.3411
Jan 1600P	100.00	0.3848	−0.4047
Jan 1650P	125.00	0.3832	−0.4691
Jan 1700P	154.00	0.3842	−0.5320
Jan 1750P	186.00	0.3853	−0.5918
Jan 1800P	221.00	0.3875	−0.6469

FIGURE 4-3
March cocoa options

Jan 1700 call is trading at 95.00 while the 1400 put is trading at 32.00. Remember from our previous discussion that we subtract the short premium from the long premium to obtain our net cost and to determine where we might make a bid or offer as the case may be for this spread.

$$95.00 - 32.00 = 63.00$$

$$63.00 \times \$10 = \$630$$

Don't forget to add your cost of trading to the position when calculating total costs.

The risk reversal can be simple to understand related to breakeven and risk if you think of it as two individual options but ordered as a spread: one long option, one short. The risk of the spread is as aggressive as the position itself. Because we have a "naked" short option, in this case the 1400 put, we have the obligation to the underlying futures at 1400, and the risk is unlimited or at least the underlying futures could conceivably go to 000. We also have the risk associated with the premium we are spending on the spread plus the costs of trading if the underlying futures are below the 17 strike price at expiration.

Calculate breakeven for the long option, as you did in for individual options, except factor in the costs from the net cost above as the premium risk on the long option position. Let's do it once together.

1700 strike price + 63 net premium = 1763 underlying futures breakeven

The short option breakeven calculation is different when you are dealing with a spread in which you have paid a premium rather than receiving a credit. In this case we must always figure the entire spread premium or net premium into the risk of the short option. Because we paid premium for the spread, we must add that premium to the strike price giving us a higher breakeven, which in turn means our risk level is closer.

1400 strike price + 63 net premium = 1463 underlying futures breakeven

AGGRESSIVE DELTA

The risk reversal can create one of the more aggressive option trades because it combines the delta of both options in the same direction. With the bull call and bear put spreads we subtract the short option delta from the long option delta; here we add the deltas together. From our example above let's look at the delta of each option and calculate the delta of the trade. Remember that even though the 1400 put has negative delta, we have shorted the position making it a long market delta.

1700 call = 0.4557   1400 put = −0.1793

0.4557 + 0.1793 = 0.635 long market delta

Therefore, with the risk reversal we have constructed a trade with a strong delta of almost two-thirds the delta of the underlying futures.

Remember, the delta of the risk reversal position will remain relatively stable until one side of the position or the other is in the money, because as one increases the other decreases.

Symbol	Price	Vlty	XDate	XDays	IRate
CCH4	1641	0.1500	12/5/03	86	5.00%

Option	Price	Imp. Vol.	Delta
Jan 1500C	200.00	0.3915	0.7065
Jan 1550C	168.00	0.3858	0.6471
Jan 1600C	141.00	0.3864	0.5835
Jan 1650C	116.00	0.3829	0.5192
Jan 1700C	95.00	0.3820	0.4557
Jan 1750C	78.00	0.3844	0.3961
Jan 1800C	63.00	0.3845	0.3397
Jan 1850C	50.00	0.3828	0.2870
Jan 1900C	40.00	0.3842	0.2414
Jan 1950C	32.00	0.3863	0.2019
Jan 2000C	25.00	0.3859	0.1659
Jan 1300P	15.00	0.3949	−0.0938
Jan 1350P	22.00	0.3912	−0.1292
Jan 1400P	32.00	0.3914	−0.1739
Jan 1450P	44.00	0.3881	−0.2236
Jan 1500P	60.00	0.3890	−0.2809
Jan 1550P	78.00	0.3856	−0.3411
Jan 1600P	100.00	0.3848	−0.4047
Jan 1650P	125.00	0.3832	−0.4691
Jan 1700P	154.00	0.3842	−0.5320
Jan 1750P	186.00	0.3853	−0.5918
Jan 1800P	221.00	0.3875	−0.6469

FIGURE 4-4
March cocoa options

Risk Reversal Put Options

The risk reversal can be constructed as a long market trade as above or a short market trade by simply buying the put option and selling the call option. The calculations are the same, so we'll just do a quick demonstration with Figure 4-4.

Here we have highlighted the sale of the 2000 call and the purchase of the 1550 put. The net premium cost here is 53. The breakeven if the trades were to expire into the underlying futures would be 1497 on the 1550 put and 1947 on the 2000 call. The combined short delta is 0.5070. If you are having trouble with these calculations, you might refer back to Chapters 2 and 3 as well as above.

Risk Reversal Advantage

The risk reversal offers the advantage of the strong delta while providing some reasonable distance from the obligation to the market from the short option position. When trading trending markets, this option spread gives the trader flexibility. The short option trade can be located at technically strategic points of support or resistance. The strong delta allows the trade to react significantly as the underlying futures move. Some traders will refer to these positions as "windows" because if the market reaches a certain point, the trader has the right to the market or increased premium to create profit potential. If the underlying futures move against the direction of the trade, the short position may be at a distance from the current market to offer the trader a better buy or sell position on the underlying futures position.

The risk reversal is a commonly used trade for market hedgers. Those who have a vested interest in the market or a product moving in one market direction may use risk reversals to apply protective stance. For example, a corn farmer may use the risk reversal instead of outright selling his crop because it provides the advantage of having the obligation to sell at a higher price than currently stated, while placing a bottom-line price as a minimum guarantee. A grain mill using corn might do the opposite, buying a call to create that maximum purchase price, while the short put ensures that their obligation to the corn will be at a lower price than the current market.

Speculators might use a risk reversal spread when following an aggressive market trend line. Intraday or intraweek volatility can often result in a trade being stopped out when using just the underlying futures. The risk reversal might allow a speculator to locate the short position outside of the recent trading range and secure aggressive delta without being too close to the current market. Remember that the risk profile of the risk reversal is aggressive. The trade has unlimited risk and unlimited profit potential.

Offsetting Prior to Expiration

As with many of the option spreads, the risk reversal's aggressive advantage provides the trader with potential opportunities to capitalize on market movement prior to expiration. With the strong delta, the underlying futures movement may quickly change the premium of the trade and create a situation to liquidate for profit or loss.

As with the bull call and bear put spread trades, the risk reversal is bid and offered as a spread. When you enter the trade, you are providing the broker with the net premium as the bid or offer. The same is true when exiting. Let's say for example that the futures moved in the favor of the put option spread above; in other words, the futures fell. Let's say the calculated net spread premium has gone from 53 to 100 because the 1550 put option is now 110 and the 2000 call option is now 10. You can then offer the spread to the market at whatever price you wish, but let's say you offer 100. The spread is bought by someone else and your position is offset. You now have a net result of 100 − 53 = 47 or $470 minus cost of trading.

If the spread were to go against you and the premium of each option has changed to where the 1550 put is worth 10 and the 2000 call is worth 100, you now must bid for the trade again to buy out your loss. The spread now costs 90 additional points to buy back. In other words you have less value in the purchased option than the short option by 90 points. You now must bid 90 for the spread instead of offering because of the short option premium. Your loss here is compounded. Not only did you lose on the purchased option premium, but also on the short option (90 + 53 = 143 or $1430 plus costs of trading).

Remember, with risk-oriented trades like this to have a risk management strategy in mind. We will discuss risk management in more detail in Chapter 6.

TEST YOUR KNOWLEDGE 4-2

1. Risk reversal trades have unlimited profit, but limited risk. True or False?
2. You must enter a risk reversal by placing each individual option separately. True or False?
3. Risk reversal is a good choice for limited-risk traders. True or False?
4. Buying the March cocoa 1750 call from Figure 4-4 and selling the March cocoa 1400 put has a net premium cost of _____.
5. Offsetting this spread at 20 on the buy would be a net result of _____.

SELL, BUY, SELL VERTICAL SPREADS

The sell, buy, sell spread combines the risk reversal and our vertical bull call or bear put spreads. This spread incorporates multiple short options against the purchased option premium. The sell, buy, sell is still a directional trade like the bull call, bear put, and risk reversal trades and incorporates a strategy of capturing option premium on both sides of the market to reduce the premium risk of a purchased option.

To create a sell, buy, sell spread for a long market position, we are looking to purchase a call option somewhere close to the money, while we sell call option farther out of the money, and sell an out-of-the-money put option as well. This capture of premium is designed to offset some of the risk of time value decay as well as reduce the sharp delta of the risk reversal in markets with more limited directional range.

Let's look at an example, Figure 4-5. Here we're looking at the Canadian dollar which like most currencies can often have pricey long-term options in which this type of trade can significantly help reduce premium cost.

In Figure 4-5, we show a three-part option spread. First we are selling the Dec 70 put, then we show the buy of the at-the-money call, the Dec 73. Finally we show the sale of the Dec 76 call to complete the sell, buy, sell spread.

Let's quickly cover our rights and obligations based on our definition of an option. We have the right, but not the obligation, to be long the underlying futures at 7300. We have the obligation to be short the underlying futures at 7600. We have the obligation to be long the underlying futures at 7000 if the option were to expire in the money.

Exercise 4-1   Let's do a quick exercise to make sure you're understanding the definition when it comes to spreads. Look at Figure 4-5 and answer the questions below. Look for the answers at the end of this chapter.

1. What do I have if the futures at option expiration are at 7420?
2. What do I have if the futures at option expiration are at 6970?
3. What do I have if the futures at option expiration are at 7845?

Let's now look at the net premium calculation of this spread. By selling the 76 call we capture 33 points; with the 70 put we capture 29 points. We now need to total the captured premium and subtract the value from the purchased option premium (73 call) of 1.20

$$120 - (33 + 29 = 62) = 58 \text{ or } \$580$$

CDZ3	0.7302	0.1500	12/5/03	82	5.00%

Option	Price	Imp. Vol.	Delta
Dec 0.7150C	2.12	0.0906	0.6876
Dec 0.7200C	1.79	0.0900	0.6301
Dec 0.7250C	1.48	0.0886	0.5694
Dec 0.7300C	1.20	0.0872	0.5052
Dec 0.7350C	0.97	0.0870	0.4401
Dec 0.7400C	0.79	0.0883	0.3787
Dec 0.7450C	0.63	0.0888	0.3208
Dec 0.7500C	0.51	0.0906	0.2706
Dec 0.7550C	0.41	0.0922	0.2262
Dec 0.7600C	0.33	0.0939	0.1883
Dec 0.7650C	0.27	0.0962	0.1574
Dec 0.6950P	-----	-----	−0.1174
Dec 0.7000P	0.29	0.0941	−0.1643
Dec 0.7050P	0.37	0.0922	−0.2022
Dec 0.7100P	0.48	0.0913	−0.2486
Dec 0.7150P	0.61	0.0901	−0.3002
Dec 0.7200P	0.77	0.0891	−0.3576
Dec 0.7250P	0.96	0.0882	−0.4192
Dec 0.7300P	1.18	0.0872	−0.4837
Dec 0.7350P	1.45	0.0874	−0.5484
Dec 0.7400P	1.77	0.0891	−0.6089

FIGURE 4-5
December Canadian dollars

Now you should run a quick breakeven calculation to see where you make money when the underlying futures expire and where you don't. We add the premium to the purchased call, which makes the futures breakeven 7358 (don't forget trading costs). On the downside risk, which is the 70 put, we have a breakeven at 7058; remember that the upside short call is covered by the 73 so it's not part of the calculation.

Our maximum profit comes in if futures exceed 7600, which would be

$$7600 - 7300 = 300 - 58 \text{ premium} = 242 \text{ or } \$2420$$

The premium risk to reward here is very good at over 4 to 1, but remember we have unlimited risk on the short put option so it should be monitored.

Short Sell, Buy, Sell

The put side of the trade is identical except that you'll construct the trade using a close-to-the-market put, selling a farther out-of-the-money put, and selling an out-of-the-money call. The risk for this trade is the same as the call side; you have unlimited risk to the short call, and you have limited profit potential on the vertical bear put spread. The calculations for profit and loss as well as breakeven are the same.

The Delta

The delta of the sell, buy, sell is reduced from the vertical risk reversal, but increased from the outright bear put or bull call spread. This is due to the short premium on both sides of the market. Often when you create a sell, buy, sell position, the two short options will have similar delta in opposite directions, which basically neutralizes the directional pressure from either option, until the market moves. The delta of the naked short option will of course increase if the market begins to move toward it. So essentially you have a delta similar to that of the outright call option but at a significantly reduced premium cost. If you look at the trade in the example, the deltas are very similar and would nearly offset. This is what you are looking for in a sell, buy, sell position.

The sell, buy, sell is commonly used in directional markets with more limited range and potential. If a market is trending in a certain direction, but the last 12 months of trading range is 30 cents, and you can sell option premium 40 or 50 cents out, the sell, buy, sell may be effective. You may be able to capitalize on the trend as well as captured premium. This trade is not as effective in fast-moving markets because of the slower delta of the short option against the market direction. The growth of premium is similar to that of the vertical bull call or bear put spreads. Use sell, buy, sell positions to reduce premium and gain market advantage in trending markets.

Remember, the sell, buy, sell has unlimited risk and limited profit potential.

Offsetting Prior to Expiration

The same rationale for managing risk or taking profits exists for the sell, buy, sell as the risk reversal spread. We are controlling the risk of risk oriented or "naked" short option premium or possibly removing the covered short option to open profit potential. We also might be removing the entire spread for risk prevention or profit taking. The sell, buy, sell position is bid and offered in a spread premium price as we have discussed. If you are managing risk or taking profits on an individual option in the spread, you can place them individually if you wish, but your premium is not set by the entire spread price. Here you would be using the premium of the individual option rather than the entire spread. Such a placement is called *legging*. If you are trying to accomplish this intraday, it may best be handled by your broker or someone with access to real-time bid offers on the exchange. This is especially true if the risk or profitability is narrow on the entire spread.

As with other spreads, calculate the premium regularly to watch for profit opportunities and make sure you have a risk management plan for the trade.

TEST YOUR KNOWLEDGE 4-3

1. Sell, buy, sell creates a limited risk spread. True or False?
2. If you do a long market sell, buy, sell, the put option is your protection. True or False?
3. You can bid or offer for a sell, buy, sell spread as a single trade, but you still have three trading costs. True or False?
4. In Figure 4-5, selling the 7000 put, buying the 7400 call, and selling the 7650 call would have a net premium cost of _____.
5. Offsetting the spread from question 4 at 110 on the sell would have a net result of _____.

RATIO CALL SPREADS

The ratio call spread is a variation on the basic bull call spread. This spread uses multiple short options to reduce the overall long option premium from the purchase. With the ratio call spread you are looking to purchase a call option relatively close or at the money while selling multiple out-of-the-money call

CLZ3	27.00	0.1500	11/17/03	56	5.00%

Option	Price	Imp. Vol.	Delta
Dec 25.50C	2.24	0.3366	0.6860
Dec 26.00C	1.90	0.3278	0.6350
Dec 26.50C	1.60	0.3226	0.5791
Dec 27.00C	1.29	0.3083	0.5201
Dec 27.50C	1.06	0.3062	0.4594
Dec 28.00C	0.88	0.3091	0.4021
Dec 28.50C	0.70	0.3052	0.3447
Dec 29.00C	0.55	0.3020	0.2907
Dec 29.50C	0.45	0.3065	0.2471
Dec 30.00C	**x2** 0.35	0.3050	0.2040
Dec 30.50C	0.25	0.2964	0.1594
Dec 23.50P	0.28	0.3508	−0.1392
Dec 24.00P	0.36	0.3448	−0.1724
Dec 24.50P	0.46	0.3396	−0.2111
Dec 25.00P	0.59	0.3372	−0.2563
Dec 25.50P	0.74	0.3335	−0.3052
Dec 26.00P	0.90	0.3259	−0.3569
Dec 26.50P	1.10	0.3217	−0.4131
Dec 27.00P	1.29	0.3083	−0.4723
Dec 27.50P	1.56	0.3071	−0.5327
Dec 28.00P	1.88	0.3110	−0.5894

FIGURE 4-6
December crude oil

options against the delta of the purchased call option. Let's look at an example in Figure 4-6 first to help illustrate this trade.

In Figure 4-6, we show the purchase of the Dec crude oil 27.00 call option with the sale of the Dec crude oil 30.00 call. Remember, crude oil is 1000 barrels quoted in dollars per barrel. Now to create the ratio call spread, we are going to increase the number of short call options in this spread. In this case we're going to go to a simple 2:1 ratio. In other words, we're selling two 30.00 calls for each 27.00 call purchased.

Let's quickly look at the premium calculation here. The 27.00 call shown above has a premium of 1.29, while the 30.00 call is showing 0.35. So we must first multiply the premium of the 30.00 call by 2.

$$0.35 \times 2 = 0.70$$

Then subtract the sum of the short calls from the purchased option premium.

$$1.29 - 0.70 = 0.59 \qquad 0.59 \times \$10 = \$590$$

We now have a combined premium of \$590 for the entire spread. Like our other spreads, the ratio call spread order is placed as a single premium for the combined total of the option premium. To relate this to our option definition: We now have the right, but not the obligation, to the underlying futures long at 27.00, and we are obligated to two contracts short at 30.00.

In order to find the breakeven of this spread, we must first calculate where we become profitable on the spread. Remember your long option breakeven for this is

$$27.00 + 0.59 \text{ (combined premium)} = 27.59$$

Anything below 27.59 would be a loss of premium and below 27.00 would be an entire loss of the invested premium plus costs of trading. Now let's look for our maximum profit potential We have the obligation at 30.00, so anything above 27.59 and below 30.00 would be profit potential as in our bull call spread.

$$30.00 - 27.59 = 2.41 \text{ or } \$2410$$

So our maximum profit is \$2410. We are however obligated to the underlying futures on two 30.00 calls. One of them, as in the bull call spread, will be completely offset by the underlying futures from 27.00, while the other will be a naked position short from 30.00.

This creates a situation where we have limited profit potential and unlimited risk to the long side of the trade, while our risk to the downside of the market is limited to the premium paid. Since we have this upside risk, we must determine the point where we begin losing profit and where the unlimited risk nature of this spread comes in.

We begin losing profit at 30.01, because the naked short option is now losing 0.01 from the 2.41 in profitable premium derived from the purchased 27.00 call. The best way to calculate the entire profit range and where you begin losing money on the spread is by adding the maximum profit calculation to the naked option strike price:

$$30.00 + 2.41 = 32.41$$

At this futures price we begin losing money on the spread again; in other words, we have now exhausted all the profit from the 27.00 call. The obligation to the 30.00 call now becomes unlimited risk to where you can lose more than the initial premium investment. Anything from 32.42 and above is outright loss.

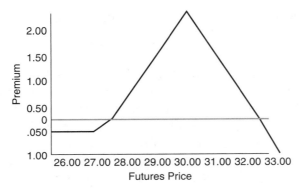

FIGURE 4-7
Option model

Figure 4-7 is a graphical representation of this trade with the option model to help illustrate the P&L of a ratio spread

You can see in Figure 4-7 how the trade begins to lose when at expiration it falls below 27.59 and reaches its maximum loss as the futures price falls to 27.00 and below. As the market rises the premium begins to rise above breakeven to a peak of profitability at 30.00. The spread premium begins to fall again after 30.00 to the upside breakeven at 32.42, and continues to fall as the futures price rises to an unlimited risk.

Ratio Spread Advantage

The ratio spread is a risk-oriented strategy that is effective in several market situations. The ratio spread is excellent for trading range-bound or technically limited range markets where above-average implied volatility is indicated on the out-of-the-money call options. This increased volatility can significantly reduce the premium paid for the spread or offset a future decrease in implied volatility and can also offset some time value decay on the purchased call option. These advantages often outweigh the risk of the spread.

To give you an example, if the recent trading range of the crude oil market we used as an example earlier has been from 25.00 to 29.00 over the past six months, then selling these out-of-the-money call options may be a very viable opportunity. The high percentage outcome would be for the 30.00 calls to expire out of the money.

The ratio spread can effectively assist you in entering markets with inflated premium. When a market has inflated option premium, purchasing at-the-money or close-to-the-money call options can be expensive and proportionately risky to the futures should the market move end quickly. The ratio spread effectively reduces the risk of the purchased premium by bringing in the OPM (other people's money) factor. This factor is especially important in option trading to offset the risk of premium expiration. We've talked about the statistics of options' expiring worthless and how buying inflated options can often be a risky strategy especially in long-term option trading. The ratio spread can effectively reduce this risk, but adds another dimension of risk from unlimited loss potential on the extra naked option.

It is often said that markets overreact by traveling higher or lower than fundamental or technical support and resistance dictate for the market price. This overreaction is where the risk of the ratio spread becomes apparent. If the market breaks the hypothetical resistance at 29.00 in our example, then the likelihood of the market traveling well beyond that resistance increases and the spread risk increases as well.

The ratio spread is a very effective long-term trading tool, and you should expect to use it in long-term situations. It is not typically effective in short-term trading because of the limited delta of the spread. This spread can be effective if you are trying to trade collapsing volatility, which you will learn more about in Chapter 5. Target your trading for expiration with this spread and be conscious of your ability to sustain the trade in high-volatility situations.

TEST YOUR KNOWLEDGE 4-4

1. A ratio spread combines a bull call spread and a sell, buy, sell trade. True or False?

2. A ratio call spread has limited risk and unlimited profit potential. True or False?

3. Ratio call spreads are excellent when using low-volatility options. True or False?

4. In high implied volatility situations ratio call spreads offer the advantage of _____.

5. In Figure 4-6, a 2:1 ratio spread buying the 2800 call and selling two 3000 calls would have premium cost of _____ and a result of _____ if the futures expired at 3040.

Ratio Put Spread

The ratio put spread is identical to the call spread only using put options. Here you are buying a closer-to-the-money put option and selling multiple put options away from the money.

The function of the spread doesn't change much either; only you must remember that you are purchasing the right to be short the underlying futures and accepting multiple obligations to be long the underlying futures at a lower price.

We'll do another quick example of the ratio spread using puts and Figure 4-8.

Figure 4-8 shows the purchase of the Dec 54 hog put with the sale of two of the Dec lean hog 48 puts.

LHZ3	54.925	0.1500	12/12/03	71	5.00%
Option	**Price**	**Imp. Vol.**	**Delta**	
Dec 52.000C	4.800	0.3376	0.6643	
Dec 53.000C	4.175	0.3332	0.6181	
Dec 54.000C	3.575	0.3265	0.5698	
Dec 55.000C	3.000	0.3174	0.5109	
Dec 56.000C	2.600	0.3214	0.4692	
Dec 57.000C	2.100	0.3096	0.4154	
Dec 58.000C	1.550	0.2863	0.3529	
Dec 59.000C	1.350	0.2963	0.3117	
Dec 60.000C	1.000	0.2831	0.2569	
Dec 61.000C	0.900	0.2970	0.2288	
Dec 62.000C	0.725	0.2970	0.1931	
Dec 48.000P	**x2** 0.850	0.3538	−0.1715	
Dec 49.000P	1.050	0.3489	−0.2045	
Dec 50.000P	1.275	0.3427	−0.2405	
Dec 51.000P	1.575	0.3411	−0.2822	
Dec 52.000P	1.875	0.3344	−0.3250	
Dec 53.000P	2.250	0.3312	−0.3719	
Dec 54.000P	2.650	0.3255	−0.4205	
Dec 55.000P	3.075	0.3174	−0.4714	
Dec 56.000P	3.675	0.3225	−0.5209	
Dec 57.000P	4.175	0.3118	−0.5740	
Dec 58.000P	4.625	0.2896	−0.6353	

FIGURE 4-8
December lean hogs

Exercise 4-2   Using your knowledge from the last section, calculate the combined premium, risk, and breakeven.

1.   What is the combined premium?
2.   To which side is the risk unlimited?

We'll do the breakeven together. The put ratio spread has limited risk to the upside and unlimited to the downside.

Premium risk plus trading costs = 0.95 or $380

Maximum profit potential =
54.00 − 48.00 − 0.95 = 5.05 or $2020 (minus trading costs)

Downside market risk = 48.00 − 5.05 = 42.95

To explain again just a bit, the risk to the upside of the market is the premium risk, which is the premium paid plus trading costs. The maximum profit potential is derived from the calculation of the distance between the strike prices minus the premium paid, which here equals 5.05. To get the downside market risk, or in other words, where we start losing money again at expiration, you subtract the profit from the ratio strike price to find the final futures price where your unlimited risk begins. In the case of puts that would be at least until zero ($17,180 plus trading costs in this case).

Remember, ratio spreads are designed to work with time decay and should not be expected to react aggressively with the market. In fact, aggressive or high volatility moves in the market may increase the out-of-the-money premium faster than the closer-to-the-money premium causing additional margin requirement and losses ahead of expiration.

THE DELTA EFFECT

We haven't discussed the delta of ratio spreads much as yet, but it is something to be very aware of especially prior to expiration. In Chapter 2, we discussed how options at or around the money are going to be about 50% in delta. An in-the-money option is going to be higher than 50% and an out-of-the-money option is likely to be lower than 50%, decreasing further as you move away from the market. Well as the market moves, these deltas change and when you are dealing with a risk-oriented spread you should be aware of the overall delta of your spread.

In Figure 4-8, we show a purchased option delta of –0.4205 and a short option delta of –0.1715. As we did in the calculation for premium, we do the same for the delta giving us a combined delta of 0.0785 or about 8% of the underlying futures movement. Since the delta increases as the market moves closer to the money, the double short options are going increase in delta as well, eventually having a higher delta than the purchased option. This demonstrates the risk we've been talking about in the fact that the short option premium can increase faster than the gains from the long option assuming no time decay has occurred yet. Just by looking at Figure 4-8, I can tell you that the delta will be about even at around 50.00 on the futures. You'll learn secret techniques to calculate delta in Chapter 6.

Estimate the delta so that you know when your ratio might be causing premium risk ahead of expiration.

MULTIPLE OPTION RATIO SPREADS

In multiple ratios the calculations are much the same, however, you must factor in the additional captured premium from all short options against the purchased option premium. This may sometimes be a credit situation where you are capturing more premium than you are paying out for the purchase option. To identify the entire spread risk you must also calculate the loss potential from all uncovered or "naked" short options.

Using the example from ratio call spreads, we demonstrated buying the 27.00 call at 1.29 and selling two 30.00 calls at .35 for a combined spread premium of .59. The breakevens in the example were 27.59 premium breakeven, and 32.41 on the topside, which we reached by taking max profit of 3.00 or $3000 minus the premium paid (.59 or $590) and added to the short strike price.

If we were to take this spread to 4:1 the 27.00 call would still be 1.29, but we would capture 1.40 in premium (.35 x 4) giving a credit of .11 or $110. So our maximum profit potential on the 4:1 ratio would now be the spread difference between 27.00 and 30.00 which is 3.00 or $3000, plus the capture premium of .11, (or $110) $3110 in total maximum profit potential.

We then have to calculate the loss potential for each short option uncovered on the risk side of the spread. Using the same example we have a total maximum profit potential of $3110 or 3.11. We now take the maximium profit and divide it by the total number of short options and add this figure to our short optionn strike price. 3.11 divided by 4 = .77, 30.00 + .77 = 30.77. So you can see that the breakeven on the 4:1 is 30.77, compared to the 32.41 on the 2:1 ratio.

TEST YOUR KNOWLEDGE 4-5

1. The unlimited risk on a ratio put spread is on the upside of the market. True or False?
2. Volatility is not a concern in the ratio put spread. True or False?
3. Multiple option ratio spreads involve a high degree of risk. True or False?
4. In Figure 4-8 the net premium of buying the 5400 put and selling three 4800 puts would be _____.
5. In question 4 the result if the futures expired at 4700 would be _____.

You must be confident of the market's limited upside potential or your ablity to sustain increased margin requirements and market losses to use multiple option ratio spreads. The advantages are certainly attractive in reduced purchase premium or even credits obtained with some risk offset from the purchased option, however be aware that prior to expiration, the multiple option ratio strategies may cause heavily increased margin requirements from your broker.

BUTTERFLY SPREADS

The butterfly spread is a nifty little evolution of the 2:1 ratio spread designed to eliminate the unlimited risk nature of the ratio. With the butterfly we'll employ the same technique as in the ratio call spread but with the addition of an out-of-the-money call or put purchase at our unlimited risk breakeven point (or close to it). With the butterfly we will be purchasing an option close to the money, while selling two options out of the money and purchasing another option an even distance from the short options as they are from the initial purchase. Confusing? Let's demonstrate using Figure 4-9.

We have highlighted the purchase of the Dec hog 56 call, the selling of two Dec hog 58 calls and the purchase of a Dec hog 60 call. You might notice from your ratio experience that the risk point for your ratio spreads is roughly the distance between the strike prices added to the short option strike price. So here, to cover that risk we have purchased a call option at that upside risk area to the ratio. Why? Let's go back to our definition of an option. You have the

LHZ3	54.925	0.1500	12/12/03	71	5.00%

Option	Price	Imp. Vol.	Delta
Dec 52.000C	4.800	0.3376	0.6643
Dec 53.000C	4.175	0.3332	0.6181
Dec 54.000C	3.575	0.3265	0.5698
Dec 55.000C	3.000	0.3174	0.5189
Dec 56.000C	2.600	0.3214	0.4692
Dec 57.000C	2.100	0.3096	0.4154
Dec 58.000C **x2** 1.550		0.2863	0.3529
Dec 59.000C	1.350	0.2963	0.3117
Dec 60.000C	1.000	0.2831	0.2569
Dec 61.000C	0.900	0.2970	0.2288
Dec 62.000C	0.725	0.2970	0.1931
Dec 48.000P	0.850	0.3538	−0.1715
Dec 49.000P	1.050	0.3489	−0.2045
Dec 50.000P	1.275	0.3427	−0.2405
Dec 51.000P	1.575	0.3411	−0.2822
Dec 52.000P	1.875	0.3344	−0.3250
Dec 53.000P	2.250	0.3312	−0.3719
Dec 54.000P	2.650	0.3255	−0.4205
Dec 55.000P	3.075	0.3174	−0.4714
Dec 56.000P	3.675	0.3225	−0.5209
Dec 57.000P	4.175	0.3118	−0.5740
Dec 58.000P	4.625	0.2896	−0.6353

FIGURE 4-9
December hogs

right to one underlying futures position at 56 and the obligation to two short at 58. If they are all in the money at expiration, you then have the profit from the 56 buy to apply against the uncovered 58 position. This runs out about 60, so we buy another right at that point to eliminate the upside risk.

Find the premiums above and let's do the calculation. The 56 call at 2.60 minus the two short 58 calls at 1.55 plus the 60 call at 1.00

$$2.60 - (1.55 \times 2) + 1.00 = 0.50 \text{ or } \$200$$

Now that we have the premium costs, let's do a breakeven analysis on this trade. Like the ratio spread the maximum profit comes in if the market expires at the short option strike price because the 56 call is 2.00 in the money while the two short option positions and the out-of-the-money call position expire worthless. This would leave us with

$$58.00 - 56.00 = 2.00 \text{ or } \$800$$

Don't forget to subtract out the initial premium, leaving you a maximum profit potential of 1.50 or $600.

Beyond the 58 point, and again like the ratio spread, the uncovered 58 call begins to take away from the profit. Our upside breakeven here is 59.50.

Short strike price + maximum profit = upside breakeven

$$58.00 + 1.50 = 59.50$$

At this point we have gained or lost nothing, except maybe cost of trading. From 59.50 to 60.00 we once again give up the initial premium of 0.50, which is the last of the 2.00 between 56 and 58. However, once we reach 60 on the underlying futures our right to be long the market kicks in and the losses are stopped at the initial premium plus costs of trading just like on the downside of the market.

This might be easier to understand with an option model as we used in the ratio spread. See Figure 4-10.

The option model demonstrates the window of profit potential created by the butterfly spread. Should the market expire in the window between 56.50 and 59.50, a profit is generated. Outside the window, the loss is limited to the premium invested plus costs of trading. The spread we demonstrate here is an acute butterfly where the range is relatively narrow and the risk to reward is 3 or 4 to 1. Obtuse butterfly spreads are more desirable and what we tend to recommend, but it varies market to market. The more obtuse the angle on your option model, the more range for profit potential. This is also often accompanied by higher premium risk.

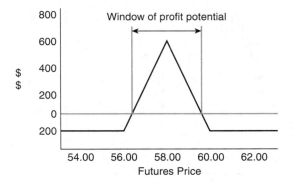

FIGURE 4-10
Option model

Butterfly Spread Advantage

The butterfly spread has a couple of distinct advantages over many option spreads. The butterfly spread creates a window of opportunity in a commodity market based on long-term trading ranges. Hypothetically, if the hog market often traded between 54.00 and 62.00, this butterfly spread might have excellent prospects for success. The butterfly spread has limited risk and many times excellent risk-to-reward ratios. This spread is an excellent choice for the investor who is looking for set-it-and-forget-it opportunities.

Let's look at the sample chart in Figure 4-11 for some ideas on using a butterfly spread.

Figure 4-11 shows four months of recent trade in the underlying futures for this market. If you look at the horizontal lines you can see the window of profit potential for the butterfly spread. In actual trading we may have chosen a larger range or more obtuse butterfly, but you can see clearly how easily range-trading markets can make butterfly spreads successful.

Butterfly spreads can also be constructed in reverse, where the trade is created for a premium credit rather than a premium debit; however, this is a much more advanced trading strategy in which you should be aware that the profit range for the position is very limited in relationship to the reward. There are other versions of butterfly spreads you may see, including those using futures

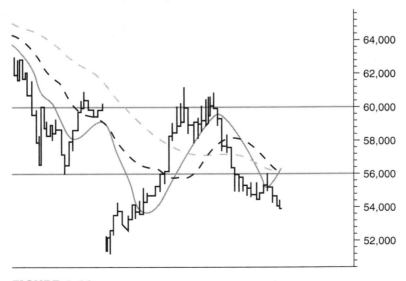

FIGURE 4-11
December hogs

which would be a calendar butterfly using different contract months to achieve gains through changes in basis.

The disadvantages for the butterfly are few, but you should be aware of them. First, you will be paying trading costs on four option transactions, so do these trades with a broker who has reasonable fees. Also, the butterfly spread is not going to take advantage of sharp market moves much like its ratio spread cousin. The delta of the trade is relatively low and may be frustrating if you see sharp market moves that you are not taking advantage of. Remember, this trade is designed to be closed out at or near expiration unless there is a specific opportunity. Lastly, the butterfly can expose you to risk if you manipulate the trade. For example, if you at some point had tremendous profits in the 56 call exampled above because the market had moved to 70.00, you would expose yourself to risk by removing the purchased options.

This disadvantage is also an advantage for the risk taker in the fact that you can play the options midway through if you understand the outright risk of short options or the increase in premium risk by buying back the short option premium.

TEST YOUR KNOWLEDGE 4-6

1. The butterfly spread has limited risk and limited reward. True or False?
2. The butterfly spread creates a window of profit potential. True or False?
3. One risk to the butterfly spread is the number of trading commissions and fees paid. True or False?
4. Butterfly spreads are effective in high implied volatility situations. True or False?
5. The example spread in Figure 4-9 would have a result of _____ if the futures expired at 6060.

BACK SPREADS

The back spread is a reversed version of the common ratio spread designed to capitalize on the vulnerabilities of the original spread. To create the back spread, we are selling an option close to the current market or even in the money and purchasing multiple options at a small distance out of the money.

This spread creates a delta situation where at the time of purchase the spread may be neutral delta or near neutral delta. As the spread matures toward expiration, market movement in the direction of the purchased options creates an increasing delta on the purchased option premium.

Let's look at an example of a back spread using a 2:1 ratio in wheat in Figure 4-12

In Figure 4-12, we show the sale of the March wheat 370 call option at a premium of 24 ¼ and the purchase of two March Wheat 390 calls at a premium of 16 ½.

The premium calculation here is the sum of the purchased option premium:

$$16 \tfrac{1}{2} \times 2 \text{ contracts} = 33$$

WH4	374 1/4	0.1500	2/20/04	141	5.00%
Option	**Price**	**Imp. Vol.**	**Delta**		
Mar 3600C	29	0.2386	0.6194	
Mar 3650C	-----	-----	0.5829	
Mar 3700C	24 1/4	0.2445	0.5494	
Mar 3750C	-----	-----	0.5153	
Mar 3800C	20	0.2478	0.4818	
Mar 3850C	-----	-----	0.4499	
Mar 3900C	**x2** 16 1/2	0.2523	0.4186	
Mar 3950C	-----	-----	0.3867	
Mar 4000C	13 5/8	0.2572	0.3613	
Mar 4050C	-----	-----	0.3276	
Mar 4100C	11 3/8	0.2638	0.3115	
Mar 3400P	7	0.2229	-0.2187	
Mar 3450P	-----	-----	-0.2624	
Mar 3500P	10 1/2	0.2297	-0.2887	
Mar 3550P	-----	-----	-0.3277	
Mar 3600P	15	0.2384	-0.3613	
Mar 3650P	-----	-----	-0.3965	
Mar 3700P	20	0.2436	-0.4315	
Mar 3750P	-----	-----	-0.4665	
Mar 3800P	25 3/4	0.2490	-0.4987	
Mar 3850P	-----	-----	-0.5355	
Mar 3900P	32 1/4	0.2556	-0.5605	

FIGURE 4-12
March Wheat

Minus the sold option premium of 24 ¼

$$33 - 24\tfrac{1}{4} = 8\tfrac{3}{4}$$

We now have a total premium outlay of 8 ¾ plus costs of trading. Let's now take a look at how the back spread creates profit and loss. As we said before, this spread reverses the shortcomings and risks of the ratio spread. The back spread is a limited risk spread although it does have unlimited profit potential

Let's look at the option model for this spread in Figure 4-13 and go through the P&L for this trade.

You can see from the model that the back spread has a very different appearance when looking at profit and loss. The trade has limited risk, but it is designed to capitalize on high volatility or sharply trending markets which have extended range. You can see by the model, with the market falling to 370 or below the amount of premium paid for the spread is the maximum loss plus cost of trading. As the market rises at expiration, the loss increases to the point of the purchased option strike price. At this point the short option is now in the money by distance to the purchased strike prices creating the maximum loss. As the market rises beyond 390, the purchased option premium increases in value offsetting the loss on the short option.

$$390 + 8\tfrac{3}{4} = 398\tfrac{3}{4} \text{ plus costs of trading}$$

At 400 the premium lost is completely offset (excepting trading costs). Beyond the 400 strike price the trade has unlimited gain potential.

Don't forget also to calculate your delta on the spread so you can be aware of the change in the spread versus the underlying futures price.

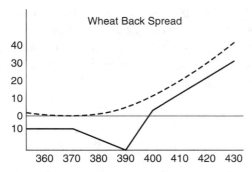

FIGURE 4-13
Option model

We sold the 370 call, which has a short delta of 0.549, while purchasing two 390 calls with an individual delta of 0.418.

$$-0.549 + (0.418 \times 2) = 0.288$$

So our overall delta is long the market by 0.288 of one futures contract.

Back Spread Advantage

The back spread is an effective option spread in situations where the market is in a low volatility position. When implied volatility on the out-of-the-money options is low, the short option premium will compensate for the majority or all of the purchase price of the two out-of-the-money options.

In using back spreads, you want to look for markets that have fundamental and technical potential to make a significant market move. An example would be applying long-term back spreads during a period prior to seasonal trends, such as heating oil or natural gas in winter, or hogs in the late spring. Markets with predictable seasonal volatility make ideal candidates for back spreads.

In addition, these spreads can be effective in markets that are at long-term lows (call back spread) or highs (put back spread). Consider that the back spread is not really designed to be held to expiration. The back spread should be considered in markets where some time prior to expiration the market is likely to make a move increasing volatility and premium. The most profitable situation for a back spread is for the market to move in your direction shortly after the trade is executed. At that point the option premium is certainly more likely to be favorable than at expiration because the purchased options are likely to have significant time value remaining. Back spreads should be considered with at least 60 days prior to expiration, but preferably 90 to 120.

The disadvantages to the back spread are limited but should be noted. Because you are purchasing option premium, many times in excess of the short option premium captured, you are at risk of the time value decaying against positive market movement, reducing profit potential. You should also be aware of the maximum risk potential of each back spread when deciding quantity of spreads. Do not exceed risk tolerance for each spread.

LONG STRANGLES

In this category of spreads we are discussing neutral delta spreads. *Neutral delta* means that in one form or another, the options utilized in the spread tend to

---

TEST YOUR KNOWLEDGE 4-7

1. Back spreads are limited risk spreads with unlimited gain potential. True or False?

2. A back spread should be applied in a market with high implied volatility. True or False?

3. If the market was at 450 for the trade in Figure 4-12, the net profit (minus trading costs) would be 51 ¼. True or False?

4. The back spread offers the market advantage of rapidly increasing delta in sharp market moves. True or False?

5. In the back spread example in Figure 4-12, if the trade were offset at a premium of 18 on the sell, the result would be _____.

---

neutralize the delta of the other options creating a spread with relatively little movement with the underlying futures. Delta changes with the futures movement; however, neutral delta spreads should have a certain range where the delta remains relatively neutral until the market weight is significantly toward one option or direction.

Up to this point in spreads we have been combining option purchases with short positions. In this spread strategy we combine purchased options to create market advantage. In a long strangle we are taking option positions on both sides of the current market.

Figure 4-14 highlights the purchase of the Nov soybean 720 call for a premium of 10 ¼ and the purchase of the Nov 660 put for a premium of 9 giving us a combined total premium of 19 ¼.

When you are doing a long strangle, you are purchasing both options at an equal distance from the market and as a spread order. This spread can be created with options at unequal distances and the calculations are the same, but for simplicity we'll demonstrate an equal distance neutral spread.

When placing the order, you would give your broker the total premium of the two purchased options.

Let's do the option breakeven calculations. In the long strangle you are spending premium for both options, so you must include this in your calculation. Let's do each side individually.

The November 720 call option gives us the right to the underlying futures long at 720. So at expiration we have a breakeven of 720 plus the spread premium of

SX3	687 1/4	0.1500	10/24/03	22	5.00%

Option	Price	Imp. Vol.	Delta	
Nov 6600C	36 1/4	0.3006	0.7186	
Nov 6700C	30	0.3057	0.6447	
Nov 6800C	24 1/2	0.3099	0.5687	
Nov 6900C	19 3/4	0.3136	0.4932	
Nov 7000C	16 1/4	0.3253	0.4233	
Nov 7100C	13	0.3307	0.3581	
Nov 7200C	10 1/4	0.3346	0.2987	
Nov 7300C	-----	-----	0.2364	
Nov 7400C	6 1/2	0.3482	0.2048	
Nov 7500C	-----	-----	0.1455	
Nov 7600C	4	0.3588	0.1356	
Nov 6200P	1 1/2	0.2886	−0.0680	
Nov 6300P	2 5/8	0.2939	−0.1069	
Nov 6400P	4 1/8	0.2953	−0.1537	
Nov 6500P	6 1/4	0.2977	−0.2115	
Nov 6600P	9	0.2992	−0.2776	
Nov 6700P	12 3/4	0.3048	−0.3520	
Nov 6800P	17 1/4	0.3096	−0.4283	
Nov 6900P	22 1/2	0.3139	−0.5038	
Nov 7000P	29	0.3259	−0.5735	
Nov 7100P	-----	-----	−0.6518	
Nov 7200P	42 7/8	0.3342	−0.6986	

FIGURE 4-14
November soybeans

19 ¼ or 739 ¼ (plus cost of trading). Everything from 739 ¼ (plus costs of trading) and above would be profit.

On the opposite side, the 660 put gives us the right to be short the underlying futures contract at the 660 strike price. Here again we must deal with the spread premium. Remember from our put option purchasing discussion that we subtract purchased premium from the strike price when dealing with put options. 660 minus 19 ¼ equals 640 ¾ (minus costs of trading). Everything from 640 ¾ and below would be profit.

Of course in each case the opposing option would expire worthless. This spread is limited risk, but should the underlying futures market expire in between the strike prices, the entire premium would be lost.

It is important to take note of the delta of this spread as well. Because we are purchasing a position on opposite sides of the market, the delta will also be opposing. The call has a long delta of 0.298 and the put has a short delta of 0.277.

$$0.298 - 0.277 = 0.021$$

This very minimal long delta will have virtually no movement with the futures market until the delta of one option begins outpacing the other. This usually occurs when one option is well in the money.

Long Strangle Advantage

The long strangle is a spread position with decidedly more disadvantages than advantages; however, it functions well for certain market situations. This spread should be considered where market volatility and implied volatility are both low, but there is anticipation in the future that volatility may increase dramatically. An increase in implied volatility will add value to the option positions as well as indicate a substantial market move. The long strangle does offer market position with limited premium or margin risk.

This spread should not be considered in any high-volatility market condition. Option values are inflated and the risk of option premium loss is high because of the distance the market must travel in order to provide profitability to the trade.

Another disadvantage is the risk of time value decay. Because you have purchased both options and have no offsetting short premium to reduce premium and time value, each day of the trade's life offers you less opportunity for the options to increase in value.

The other major risk to this spread is order entry. As we said above, the spread should be entered as a spread order. You can always leg into a spread of this nature by doing one option then the other, but typically you would want to do both at the same time to avoid any market changes which would unbalance the spread.

Legging out of the spread is a possibility when markets are cycling significantly. Should the market fall with a future expectation of recovery, profits could be taken on one side and risk the balance of the premium to the opposing option. You might think of this as ending up with one option for "free." If the profit on one side is enough to compensate for the entire premium spent, then the remaining option has zero risk. In deep cycling markets, this is a highly effective trading strategy.

TEST YOUR KNOWLEDGE 4-8

1. A long strangle is an excellent high-volatility market position. True or False?

2. A major risk for long strangle positions is time value decay. True or False?

3. An increase in implied volatility may benefit a long strangle. True or False?

4. Buying a long strangle the day before a government report would have _____ risk.

5. The Long strangle might be offset by legging to accomplish _____.

SHORT STRANGLES

The short strangle reverses the situation of the long strangle. Here we are selling options on both sides of the market. In other words we are selling out-of-the-money call and put options at relatively equal distances from the current market price.

The major differences in the spreads come in the risk profile of the trade and in the reversal of the time value risk. In the long strangle our risk is limited to the premium spent; however, it is considered significant because of the purchase of both options. In the short strangle we reverse the risk to an unlimited risk situation because we are short options on both sides of the market.

The short strangle takes advantage of the major shortcoming of the long strangle, the time value decay and premium spent. Because we are offering the options, we reverse the situation and take in the premium from the buyer. If the options were to expire worthless, we capture the entire premium from the buyer. The buyer's risk is the seller's advantage and vice versa.

Let's look at Figure 4-14 again. The highlighted Nov soybean 720 call for a premium of 10 ¼ and the Nov 660 put for a premium of 9 gives us a combined total premium of 19 ¼. Only this time we are capturing this premium from selling these options rather than paying out for the premium.

When you are doing a short strangle opposite of the long strangle, you are selling both options at an equal distance from the market and as a spread order. Also, like the long strangle we can create this spread at unequal distances from the current market, but we'll use a simple example.

Let's do the option breakeven calculations for the short side. In the long strangle you are spending premium for both options; in the short strangle you are taking in premium as you would when selling an outright option.

The November 720 call option gives us the obligation to the underlying futures short at 720. So at expiration we have a breakeven of 720 minus the spread premium of 19 ¼ or 739 ¼ (plus cost of trading). Everything from 739 ¼ (minus costs of trading) and above would be a loss.

On the opposite side, the 660 put gives us the obligation to be long the underlying futures contract at the 660 strike price. 660 minus 19 ¼ equals 640 ¾ (plus costs of trading). Everything from 640 ¾ and below would be a loss.

Let's look at the option model in Figure 4-15 of the short strangle to help you understand the profit potential. This model is exaggerated in size.

Short Strangle Advantage

Reversing the situation of a long strangle puts the advantage of time value decay and implied volatility on your side. Short strangles should be used in high implied volatility situations where time value is on your side. We are looking for markets that have excessive premium because of market volatility. Typically these spreads should be used where fundamental and technical features of the market are more ascertainable. We often recommend theses spreads at 90 days or less to expiration.

The risk comes in the unlimited loss feature of the trade. Should the underlying futures market exceed the strike price on either side of the market, the loss can be substantial in relation to the profit potential.

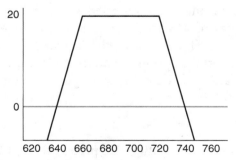

FIGURE 4-15
Option model

The short strangle can be created as a neutral delta spread by using the delta calculations we learned in previous discussions.

LONG STRADDLES

The long straddle position emulates the long strangle except that the strike price arrangement is different. The straddle name is exactly what this type of neutral delta option spread does. It straddles the market by buying a put and a call option at the same strike price at the same time.

By executing a straddle you have market position no matter which direction the underlying futures market travels because you are long an option in either direction. This is a limited risk spread because we are purchasing both options. The entire premium plus costs of trading is at risk.

Let's look at Figure 4-16 to get a clear picture of this trade; then we'll go through the advantages and disadvantages of the spread

In Figure 4-16 we show the purchase of the Dec 30 U.S. Treasury 112 call at $2\ ^{25}\!/_{64}$ and the purchase of the Dec 30 U.S. Treasury 112 put at $2\ ^{21}\!/_{64}$.

We need to do some addition here and add the premiums together to get our combined premium costs.

$$2\ ^{25}\!/_{64} + 2\ ^{21}\!/_{64} = 4\ ^{46}\!/_{64}$$

$$4\ ^{46}\!/_{64} \times \$1000 = \$4718.75$$

We can now calculate the breakeven for this position. Now, remember because we are combining premium here, the breakeven for the position must include the combined premium.

Before we can do that we need a quick financial lesson on using options with Treasury instruments. Treasury futures are reported with a tick size of $^{1}\!/_{32}$, while the futures are quoted as a tick of $^{1}\!/_{64}$. Each full point of movement is the same at $1000 per point as we demonstrated above, the instrument quoting is just different. So we must first convert the option premium into 32ds. This is a simple matter of dividing the numerator and denominator by 2. Leave the whole numbers alone because they are full points:

$$^{46}\!/_{64} \div 2 = {}^{23}\!/_{32}$$

Now we can look at the breakeven. Both strike prices are at 112. We add the premium to the call option so that the call side would be $112 + 4\ ^{23}\!/_{32}$ or $116\ ^{23}\!/_{32}$. This would be the upside breakeven at expiration.

USZ3	112 2/32	0.1500	11/21/03	50	5.00%
Option	**Price**	**Imp. Vol.**	**Delta**		
Dec 10900C	4 17/64	0.1512	0.6948		
Dec 11000C	3 37 /64	0.1485	0.6383		
Dec 11100C	2 61/64	0.1461	0.5766		
Dec 11200C	2 25/64	0.1436	0.5113		
Dec 11300C	1 59/64	0.1429	0.4448		
Dec 11400C	1 33/64	0.1420	0.3795		
Dec 11500C	1 11/64	0.1410	0.3172		
Dec 11600C	58/64	0.1414	0.2614		
Dec 11700C	43/64	0.1402	0.2091		
Dec 11800C	32/64	0.1404	0.1654		
Dec 11900C	23/64	0.1397	0.1271		
Dec 10500P	28/64	0.1599	−0.1285		
Dec 10600P	37/64	0.1580	−0.1623		
Dec 10700P	48/64	0.1557	−0.2016		
Dec 10800P	61/64	0.1526	−0.2460		
Dec 10900P	1 13/64	0.1497	−0.2968		
Dec 11000P	1 33/64	0.1476	−0.3542		
Dec 11100P	1 57/64	0.1456	−0.4164		
Dec 11200P	2 21/64	0.1436	−0.4819		
Dec 11300P	2 55/64	0.1433	−0.5482		
Dec 11400P	3 29/64	0.1429	−0.6128		
Dec 11500P	4 7/64	0.1424	−0.6742		

FIGURE 4-16
30-year treasury bonds

For the put the scenario is $112 - 4\,^{23}/_{32}$ or $107\,^9/_{32}$

On the Internet or quote system you'll mostly see these quoted as 107-09 or 107.09. Just remember that this means $107\,^9/_{32}$.

Figure 4-17 is an option model for this trade.

You can see in the model that the option position has money-making potential in either direction the underlying futures market travels. There are, however, some distinct disadvantages to the long straddle.

First, this spread must be applied in low implied volatility situations. If implied volatility is high, you are paying inflated prices for two options. The likelihood of volatility increasing when it is already high is definitely decreased. It is very

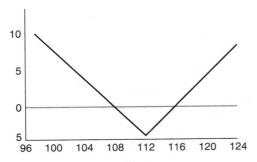

FIGURE 4-17
Option model

important to find a low volatility situation where it is likely that your premium will expand because of increased volatility as well as market movement.

If you were to apply a long straddle spread and the bond market referenced above were to quickly move 4 to 6 points in one direction you may see a significant increase in premium on one side of the spread making it possible to take profit on the entire spread from increased volatility and from the change in delta from market movement.

Second, you need time with this option spread. The theory here is to take advantage of market cycles or extreme market movement. It is often the case that markets move in cycles, and not necessarily trend, so that you can apply a spread of this nature and with market movement take profit on one side of the spread. Allow the cycle to complete and recover premium or take profit on the remaining side. To do this, you need to avoid the dramatic time value decay from short-term options. You should look for options with at least 120 days till expiration unless you are playing a particular event such as a government report or seasonal trade.

The major disadvantage is time decay; each day the options are worth something less than the previous day in time value. Remember this and consider it carefully when using this type of spread.

Exercise 4-3   Take the 110 strike price from Figure 4-16 and create a long straddle. Calculate your breakeven and then answer the questions below. Make sure you convert to 32ds and draw your model.

1. What is the total premium?

2. With expiration at a futures price of 110, the loss would be $4725 plus cost of trading. True or False?

3. The call breakeven for this trade would be _____.

Delta Strategy

Typically straddles should be applied at the money or somewhere near the current futures price. This ensures the neutral delta of the spread. As we've learned delta tends to be near 50% when the strike price is at the money.

The natural tendency of people to be bullish tends to lead to more available strike prices in call options than put options. This can lead to a slight skew in volatility and actual delta performance between calls and puts at equal distances from the market. Since the straddle, especially the long straddle relies on volatility and overall option performance, it is important to keep this difference in mind and work as close to the market on straddles as possible. Some traders will even apply straddles in the money on one side to reduce the total time value risk by applying an option that has significant intrinsic value. Just be aware that should the market not perform as expected there is significant premium at stake.

SHORT STRADDLES

We'll now look at the reverse of the long straddle by selling both options rather than buying. We call this the short straddle and it involves selling a put and a call in the same contract month and at the same strike price as we did in the long straddle.

In the short straddle you are accepting the risk and advantages opposite of the long straddle—meaning that the trade is unlimited in risk on either side of the market. The advantage comes from the time value and/or volatility decay from two high-delta options

We want to use the same example from our long straddle because technically this particular spread is something that can be utilized effectively in a short straddle or a long straddle based on historical market movement. Let's first run quickly through the trade using Figure 4-16 and breakevens again; then we'll look at a chart to see the effectiveness of the straddle. Remember this time we are using this spread as a short straddle, meaning selling both options.

In Figure 4-16 we show the sale of the Dec 30 U.S. Treasury 112 call at 2 $\frac{25}{64}$ and the purchase of the Dec 30 U.S. Treasury 112 put at 2 $\frac{21}{64}$.

The breakeven analysis is the same as we used with the purchased straddle, or long straddle.

$$2 \tfrac{25}{64} + 2 \tfrac{21}{64} = 4 \tfrac{46}{64}$$

$$4\ {}^{46}\!/_{64} \times \$1000 = \$4718.75$$

Both strike prices are at 112; starting with the call option we add the premium and the call side would be 112 + 4 ${}^{23}\!/_{32}$ or 116 ${}^{23}\!/_{32}$. This would be the upside breakeven at expiration.

For the put the scenario the breakeven is 112 − 4 ${}^{23}\!/_{32}$ or 107 ${}^{9}\!/_{32}$

Don't forget costs of trading. So, when you are shorting the options above you now have a profit range from 107–109 to 116–123. If the futures were to expire anywhere in this area, you would show a profit (minus costs of trading). Outside of this range, the loss is unlimited.

Now let's look at a real-world scenario using the weekly chart and the numbers above. This was a Dec '03 option, so let's look at the chart we have in Figure 4-18 where these options expired and what the historical range was for this trade.

The shaded area on the chart roughly represents the range of the straddle referenced. In this particular example you can see the majority of the market

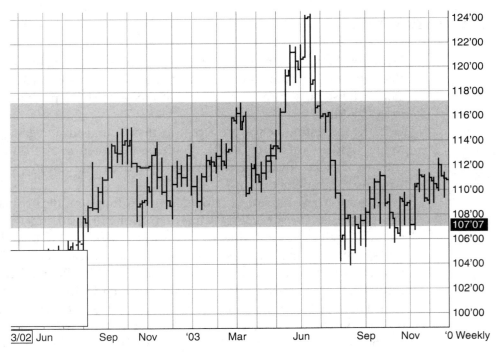

FIGURE 4-18
30-year treasury bond

time from mid-2002 through the end of 2003 was spent inside this range. There were spikes and drops which might have been effective points for the long straddle as well if the trader had targets set for profit taking on each side of the position. It is most likely that the short straddle would have been most effective for this market during this time frame.

Looking at the actual trade referenced above it was placed roughly the first week of October and was set to expire the third week of November. You can see that the market remained in the range through the entire time frame excepting one week, and the trade would have ended with the call option expired and the put option barely in the money for an immediate offset.

The short strategy would have been most successful here, but given the right circumstances, a sharp change in market direction can lead to deep market trends. Soybeans and grains in general are notorious for range trading except for those serious fundamental changes which cause deep long-term market trends. Much of this is based on massive anticipated supply changes due to weather or crop conditions. Livestock is another excellent example of markets that can be very effective for these spreads. Premiums run high and high volatility is not unusual.

Each market is different when it comes to strategy and risk management. Remember when you are dealing with a short straddle or strangle position you are in an unlimited risk position. Managing this risk is covered in more detail in Chapter 6, but it is certain to say you should have a definitive plan for managing short option risk just as you would with an outright futures position, long or short. It is important to remember risk to reward when selling options. It is also important to remember that the short strangle and straddle positions develop margin requirement from the applicable exchange or clearing house. You should keep in mind the ability to financially sustain this type of risk when evaluating margin and trade suitability.

CREDIT SPREADS

Our next discussion is on another evolution of short option trading where we manage risk by using a purchased option. With credit spread we are looking for a market which may be too volatile to justify an outright option position or a market which may present to much monetary risk to work with an outright option position.

The credit spread is created by selling an option position closer to the current market and buying an option further from the market in the same direction (i.e., call or put). Let's look at an example in Figure 4-19.

In Figure 4-19 we show the sale of the Dec S&P 500 1040 call and the purchase of the Dec S&P 500 1050 call. The S&P 500 contracts' value is based on a multiple of the index. In this case it's what we call the "big board" meaning the full futures as compared to the e-mini contract which is one-fifth the size. The S&P is $250 times the index price. So if the S&P is at 1000.00, it represents an S&P 500 stock portfolio value of $250,000. The futures and options are $250 per full point. The e-mini S&P would be $50 times the index. Again,

SPZ3 1016.40 Exp 12/19/03 DTE 78			
Option	Price	Imp. Vol.	Delta
Dec 1000.00	46.60	0.2063	0.5802
Dec 1005.00	43.60	0.2045	0.5601
Dec 1010.00	40.50	0.2016	0.5397
Dec 1015.00	37.60	0.1992	0.5188
Dec 1020.00	34.80	0.1968	0.4973
Dec 1025.00	32.10	0.1944	0.4754
Dec 1030.00	29.60	0.1925	0.4534
Dec 1035.00	27.20	0.1905	0.4311
Dec 1040.00	25.00	0.1891	0.4090
Dec 1045.00	22.80	0.1870	0.3864
Dec 1050.00	20.60	0.1842	0.3633
Dec 980.00P	23.90	0.2159	−0.3354
Dec 985.00P	25.40	0.2136	−0.3529
Dec 990.00P	26.90	0.2108	−0.3709
Dec 995.00P	28.60	0.2086	−0.3898
Dec 1000.00P	30.30	0.2059	−0.4091
Dec 1005.00P	32.20	0.2038	−0.4291
Dec 1010.00P	34.10	0.2012	−0.4496
Dec 1015.00P	36.20	0.1991	−0.4706
Dec 1020.00P	38.40	0.1970	−0.4920
Dec 1025.00P	40.70	0.1949	−0.5138
Dec 1030.00P	43.10	0.1927	−0.5359

FIGURE 4-19
December SP500

if the market was at 1000, the value would be $50,000. Let's now look at the option premium.

We are selling the 1040 call for a premium of 25.00 or $6250

$$25.00 \times \$250 = \$6250$$

We are purchasing the 1050 call for premium of 20.60 or $5150

$$20.60 \times \$250 = \$5150$$

Therefore, our net premium is 4.40 or $1100 minus cost of trading.

Let's look at our breakeven and risk calculation. We are taking the obligation to the underlying futures at 1040 and buying the right to the underlying futures at 1050. For this risk we are accepting the premium of 4.40 which is our maximum profit. We find our breakeven just as we have with all short options by taking the strike price and adding the captured premium.

$$1040 + 4.40 = 1044.40$$

Our breakeven on the underlying futures is now 1044.40, so anything above that point (don't forget to subtract costs of trading) would be loss.

The purchase option comes in to define our risk. Because we have the right to the underlying futures at 1050, we now can offset the risk of the 1040 call at 1050. With the right to the futures at 1050, should the underlying futures be higher than 1050 at the time of expiration, you can assume the futures at 1050 and offset the futures accepted at 1040.

$$1050 - 1040 = 10.00 \text{ maximum spread risk}$$

$$10.00 - 4.40(\text{captured premium}) = 5.60 \text{ maximum trade risk}$$

We now have a limited risk position with a maximum risk of $1400. The credit spread is an excellent means of trading markets with an unacceptable level of risk.

Credit Spread Advantage

The strategy for this type of spread is to look for markets in which the short option premium is likely out of the intended trading range but may be close enough to generate a significant amount of premium. This type of spread is often most effective in high-value markets such as the S&P, Treasury bonds, and currency.

It is not typically as effective in markets like the grains because of the low variance in premium between strike prices. The risk often outweighs the premium by a significant factor. A credit spread should not be applied where the reward or captured premium is a quarter or less the total spread risk. It is preferred that it is a third or greater.

You also might look for markets in which the volatility variance between strike prices does not significantly affect the trade. In other words, a sharp rise in implied volatility in out-of-the-money strike prices might indicate that the purchased premium is overvalued and may negate profitability.

The credit spread is a very effective limited risk tool in option trading and can be part of a broader risk management strategy.

CONDOR SPREADS

The condor spread is the ultimate evolution of the credit spread. The condor incorporates all of the risk and reward of the credit spread from our last section, only on both sides of the market. This brings in additional premium without increasing the maximum risk. Let's use the S&P 500 again to illustrate in Figure 4-20. We have added a credit spread on the put side of the market to complete the condor.

In Figure 4-20 we show the spread from the previous example of selling the 1040 call while buying the 1050 call in the Dec S&P 500 (Chicago Mercantile Exchange). Remember the premium captured totaled 4.40 or $1100. Now we have added a credit spread on the put side selling the 990 put and buying the 980 put. The spread difference in strike prices is the same at 10 points.

Looking at the premium calculation for the put spread, we can see a premium capture of 3.00 points. If you're having trouble with the calculation, refer back to the credit spread discussion.

Let's now look at the combined premium. Remember that we are capturing from both sides of the market and we can add this premium together as we did in our short straddles and strangles. Essentially that is what a condor is, a limited-risk short strangle

From the call spread we captured 4.40, the put 3.00.

Our total premium capture is 7.40. What does this do to our breakeven calculation? We can add the combined premium to the short strike price.

So if the call side of the short was in the money, the breakeven would be 1047.40 (1040 + 7.40) and our maximum risk is now 2.60 plus cost of trading.

SPZ3 1016.40 Exp 12/19/03 DTE 78			
Option	Price	Imp. Vol.	Delta
Dec 1000.00	46.60	0.2063	0.5802
Dec 1005.00	43.60	0.2045	0.5601
Dec 1010.00	40.50	0.2016	0.5397
Dec 1015.00	37.60	0.1992	0.5188
Dec 1020.00	34.80	0.1968	0.4973
Dec 1025.00	32.10	0.1944	0.4754
Dec 1030.00	29.60	0.1925	0.4534
Dec 1035.00	27.20	0.1905	0.4311
Dec 1040.00	25.00	0.1891	0.4090
Dec 1045.00	22.80	0.1870	0.3864
Dec 1050.00	20.60	0.1842	0.3633
Dec 980.00P	23.90	0.2159	−0.3354
Dec 985.00P	25.40	0.2136	−0.3529
Dec 990.00P	26.90	0.2108	−0.3709
Dec 995.00P	28.60	0.2086	−0.3898
Dec 1000.00P	30.30	0.2059	−0.4091
Dec 1005.00P	32.20	0.2038	−0.4291
Dec 1010.00P	34.10	0.2012	−0.4496
Dec 1015.00P	36.20	0.1991	−0.4706
Dec 1020.00P	38.40	0.1970	−0.4920
Dec 1025.00P	40.70	0.1949	−0.5138
Dec 1030.00P	43.10	0.1927	−0.5359

FIGURE 4-20
December SP500

On the put side of the equation the breakeven would be 982.60 with again a maximum spread risk of 2.60 plus cost of trading.

The advantage is that the market can only expire through one side of the spread, so one side will always expire worthless leaving the entire premium from that side of the spread as gain.

The condor spread is highly effective in high-margin, high-value markets like the credit spread. The disadvantage to the condor spread is the high number of trading commissions and fees involved with four option trades. In addition you may find significant margin requirements in markets like the S&P 500, check with your broker for information on the margin involved.

A condor is also sometimes referred to as a *butterfly* when you are combining credit spreads that end up being a straddle at one strike price rather than a strangle at different strike prices.

KEY SPREAD STRATEGIES AND TERMS

Back spread Sell call lower strike, buy multiple calls higher strike or sell put higher strike, buy multiple puts lower strike.

Bear put spread Buy put higher strike, sell put lower strike.

Bull call spread Buy call lower strike sell call higher strike.

Butterfly spread Buy call lower strike, sell two calls higher strike, buy one call even higher strike or buy put higher strike, sell two put lower strike; can be reversed for credit spread.

Condor Opposing credit spreads

Credit spread Sell call lower strike, buy call higher strike or sell put higher strike, buy put lower strike.

Long straddle Buy call, buy put same strike price.

Long strangle Buy call, buy put different strike prices.

Neutral delta Option spread positions in which the opposing delta cancels to near or at zero.

Ratio call spread Buy call lower strike, sell multiple calls higher strike.

Ratio put spread Buy put higher strike, sell multiple puts lower strike.

Risk reversal Sell put, buy call or sell call, buy put

Sell, buy, sell Sell put, buy call lower strike, sell call higher strike or sell call, buy put higher strike, sell put lower strike.

Short straddle Sell call, sell put same strike price.

Short strangle Sell call, sell put different strike prices

CHAPTER TEST

1. Which of the following is not an advantage of a bull call or bear put spread?

   (a) Limited risk

   (b) Unlimited profit potential

   (c) Reduced premium outlay

   (d) Market position

2. Which spread offers the advantage of limited risk?

   (a) Risk reversal

   (b) Long straddle

   (c) Sell, buy, sell

   (d) Short strangle

3. A credit spread on each side of the market creates what position?

   (a) Butterfly spread

   (b) Sell, buy, sell

   (c) Condor spread

   (d) Back spread

4. If you purchase the 230 corn call and sell the 260 corn call at a spread premium of 0.15 your maximum profit potential is _____, assuming trade costs of $50 per round turn.

   (a) 30

   (b) 45

   (c) 25

   (d) 13

5. Which of the following has all necessary information to properly communicate an order to your broker?

   (a) Buy 1 March Japanese Yen 100 call, sell 2 March Japanese Yen 103 call, 20 on the buy for the day.

   (b) Buy 1 March Japanese Yen call, sell 2 March Japanese Yen calls at 20 GTC

   (c) None of the above

6. Which best describes the back spread?

    (a) Limited risk, unlimited profit potential, high premium risk.

    (b) Limited risk, limited profit potential, low premium risk

    (c) Unlimited risk, limited profit potential, premium credit

    (d) None of the above

7. Which best describes the bull call spread?

    (a) Limited risk, unlimited profit potential, high premium risk.

    (b) Limited risk, limited profit potential, low premium risk

    (c) Unlimited risk, limited profit potential, premium credit

    (d) None of the above

8. Which best describes the short straddle?

    (a) Limited risk, unlimited profit potential, high premium risk.

    (b) Limited risk, limited profit potential, low premium risk

    (c) Unlimited risk, limited profit potential, small premium credit

    (d) Unlimited risk, limited profit potential, risk on both sides

9. Creating the sell, buy, sell you are:

    (a) Selling 2 puts, buying 1 call

    (b) Selling 1 put, buying 1 call, selling 1 more put

    (c) Selling 1 put, buying 1 call, selling 1 call

    (d) Selling 1 call, buying 2 puts, selling 1 put

10. High implied volatility is a negative for which of the following?

    (a) Back spread

    (b) Long straddle

    (c) Long strangle

    (d) All of the above

ANSWERS TO TESTS

Test Your Knowledge 4-1

1. True. Remember to subtract purchased option premium from short option premium $(2.04 - 1.00 = 1.04)$. 2. False. Remember the purchased option is pos-

itive delta, the short option is negative delta, so you would add negative value or simply subtract short delta from long. 3. True. Don't forget to subtract the premium paid for the spread of 0.54 or $540. Maximum profit potential $460. 4. $1290 (147 − 76 = 71) (3300 − 3100 = 200) (200 − 71 = 129) (129 × $10 = $1290). 5. $300.

Test Your Knowledge 4-2

1. False. This trade is unlimited profit potential, and also unlimited risk. 2. False. The risk reversal can be entered individually, but to ensure proper premium enter it as a spread. 3. False. This is an aggressive profile trade, not for traders with limited risk profiles. 4. 46 (78 − 32 = 46) × $10 = 460. 5. 46 +20 = 66 or $660

Test Your Knowledge 4-3

1. False. The sell, buy, sell is limited profit, unlimited risk. 2. False. The put option in a long sell buy sell is naked short, meaning unlimited risk. 3. True. You may bid or offer for the spread at one premium, but you still have three trading costs, one for each option. 4. 23 or $230 [79 − (29 + 23) = 23]. 5. 110 − 23 = 77 or $770.

Test Your Knowledge 4-4

1. False. The ratio call spread is the purchase of a closer-to-the-money call, with the sale of multiple call options out of the money. 2. False. The ratio call spread is limited in risk to the downside of the market, but unlimited to the upside and limited profit. 3. False. This spread is best used in higher implied volatility situations. 4. Inflated premium captured on short options. 5. 70 − (35 × 2) = 0, 3000 − 2800 = 200, 200 − 40 = 160 × $10 = $1600.

Test Your Knowledge 4-5

1. False. The naked short option is to the short side or downside of the market; this is where the unlimited risk comes in. 2. False. Volatility is one of the risks

of a ratio spread in that the short options may increase in value faster than the purchased option. 3. True. Multiple option ratios involve a high degree of risk and should be monitored closely. 4. $2.65 - (3 \times 0.85) = 0.10 \times \$400 = \$40$. 5. $5400 - 4800 = 6.00$ long option profit. $4800 - 4700 = 1.00 \times 3 = 3.00$ short option loss. $6.00 - 3.00 = 3.00 \times \$400 = \$1200$.

Test Your Knowledge 4-6

1. True. The butterfly is limited in profit and limited in risk to the premium and fees. 2. True. The window of opportunity is between the premium breakeven and the upside breakeven (downside if it's a put spread). 3. True. Always keep trading commissions in mind in all trading. 4. True. High volatility equals inflated premium. 5. Loss of 0.50 premium.

Test Your Knowledge 4-7

1. True. The spread offers the advantage of limited risk and unlimited gain. 2. False. Remember to use this spread when implied volatility is low on the purchased options. 3. True. $450 - 398 \frac{3}{4} = 51 \frac{1}{4}$. 4. True. Multiple options create potential for higher delta. 5. $18 - 8.75 = 9.25 \times \$50 = 462.50$

Test Your Knowledge 4-8

1. False. High implied volatility means inflated option premium which is a major risk of this spread. 2. True. Time value decay works against purchased options each day, with both options purchased this risk is accelerated. 3. True. Increasing volatility tends to increase option value, which in turn could increase the overall value of the spread. 4. A neutral or unsurprising report might cause a large drop in implied volatility and create a loss of premium. 5. Profit on one side allows for lower cost or free trade of the remaining option.

Exercise 4-1

1. Long 1 December Canadian Dollar future from 7300.
2. Long 1 December Canadian Dollar future from 7000.

3. Long 1 December Canadian Dollar future from 7300, Short 1 future from 7600. Gain of 300 minus initial premium and costs of trading.

Exercise 4-2

1. $2.65 - (0.85 \times 2) = 0.95$ $0.0095 \times 40,000$ lbs = $365
2. The unlimited risk is to the downside because of the uncovered short put.

Exercise 4-3

1. Total Premium $5125. ($1 - 33 + 3 - 37 = 5 \, ^{6}/_{32}$ or $5125)
2. False. The maximum loss is the paid premium plus cost of trading $5125.
3. Call breakeven 115 03 ($110 + 5 \, ^{3}/_{32} = 115 - 03$).

Chapter Test

1. b. Profit potential in bear put and bull call spreads is limited by the short option.
2. b. The long straddle is limited risk because both options are purchased.
3. c. The condor spread is created with two opposing credit spreads
4. d. $(260 - 230 = 30)(30 - 15$ premium $= 15)(15 - 1$ trade costs $= 14)$
5. a. Choice b is missing the strike price.
6. a. The back spread has unlimited profit potential and limited risk, but the premium risk or time value risk is very high.
7. b. Bull call spreads have limited risk and profit potential and typically lower risk of time value decay and lower premium.
8. d. Although *c* is also possibly correct, *d* is the better answer with the risk on both sides of the market.
9. c. This is the proper 1:1 sell, buy, sell.
10. d. All of these are susceptible to larger premium risk in higher implied volatility situations.

CHAPTER 5

ADVANCED STRATEGY

In this chapter we'll be focusing on more advanced option and option spread strategies. We'll be covering:

- Multiple option strategy
- Calendar spreads
- Delta strategy
- Volatility strategy
- Combining futures and options

MULTIPLE OPTION STRATEGY

This is a very tricky area of advanced option trading. This strategy involves buying multiple out-of-the-money option positions, call or put, rather than closer to the market options. You'll see brokers or trading advisers recommending a large multiple option position in advertising or promotional material. "Buy 5 gold calls today...etc." You've probably heard or seen the ads on TV or radio and maybe you've received some of these recommendations in the mail.

This discussion is designed to help you break down fact from fiction and real option strategy from positions designed to separate you from your money in commission and trading fees, not to mention the premium risk.

There are without question numerous success stories of those buying a bunch of out-of-the-money call or put options and "bang" making thousands upon thousands in profit. Unfortunately, there are a far greater number of stories of total losses on these positions. Because of the heavy losses incurred regulators have cracked down on promotions for this trading style. How do you determine what is solid trading strategy and what is likely to burn commissions and premium?

First, let's say hypothetically your futures analysis tells you that a particular market has upside potential. You decide to go with a limited risk strategy of a call option rather than the futures or selling put premium. Let's look at the option table in Figure 5-1 and choose our strategy.

Buying the at-the-money call option in the Dec Canadian dollar would be the 73.00 call. The premium cost involved here is 1.20 or $10 × 1.20 or $1200.

CDZ3	0.7302	0.1500	12/5/03	82	5.00%
Option	**Price**	**Imp. Vol.**	**Delta**		
Dec 0.7150C	2.12	0.0906	0.6876		
Dec 0.7200C	1.79	0.0900	0.6301		
Dec 0.7250C	1.48	0.0886	0.5694		
Dec 0.7300C	1.20	0.0872	0.5052		
Dec 0.7350C	0.97	0.0870	0.4401		
Dec 0.7400C	0.79	0.0883	0.3787		
Dec 0.7450C	0.63	0.0888	0.3208		
Dec 0.7500C	0.51	0.0906	0.2706		
Dec 0.7550C	0.41	0.0922	0.2262		
Dec 0.7600C	0.33	0.0939	0.1883		
Dec 0.7650C	0.27	0.0962	0.1574		
Dec 0.6950P	-----	-----	−0.1174		
Dec 0.7000P	0.29	0.0941	−0.1643		
Dec 0.7050P	0.37	0.0922	−0.2022		
Dec 0.7100P	0.48	0.0913	−0.2486		
Dec 0.7150P	0.61	0.0901	−0.3002		
Dec 0.7200P	0.77	0.0891	−0.3576		
Dec 0.7250P	0.96	0.0882	−0.4192		
Dec 0.7300P	1.18	0.0872	−0.4837		
Dec 0.7350P	1.45	0.0874	−0.5484		
Dec 0.7400P	1.77	0.0891	−0.6089		
Dec 0.7450P	-----	-----	−0.6661		

FIGURE 5-1
December Canadian

The delta of the at-the-money call here is listed at just over 50%. So if we purchase one of these options, we now have a maximum risk of 1.20 plus cost of trading.

Looking at multiple options for around the same dollar expenditure, we can see the 7600 call would allow us to buy approximately four options. The 76 call at a premium of 0.33 or $330 per option. Four options would be $1320 plus costs of trading. The delta of the 76 call option is 0.188 or 18.8%. Multiplying this times four options would give you a combined delta of 75.2%. This is an advantage over the at-the-money call purchase. The larger delta means a more rapid premium growth as the futures move.

So far we've analyzed that the delta of the multiple option position is better and the premium is very similar. It all sounds good so far, but we have to look at the potential of this market during the most recent history. For this we'll go to a standard bar chart and look at the past trading history, current trend, and how the market stacks up against the call option. We're going to use the actual chart captured from Barchart.com, which we show in Figure 5-2, for the options referenced to demonstrate, but remember this does not imply a trading recommendation; it is strictly for historical reference.

Special Trading Tip This can be a fantastic learning tool: When you're looking at a hypothetical trading recommendation or the "If I had only bought…," take a piece of blank paper and put it over the history of the chart on your screen or paper up to the date on which you "should have" and then look at it again. Would you have made that decision? Be honest with yourself. It'll make you a much better trader and help you look for key signs of market direction and changes earlier in chart cycles.

In Figure 5-2 we're showing you the daily chart up until the options above were captured from a spreadsheet. You can see a nice upward trend, but the market was not trading anywhere near the 76 mark and hadn't in the last couple months. Now let's add a weekly look to our analysis in Figure 5-3.

The chart shows a little better history of the Canadian dollar and it has approached the 76 mark, but not yet been to it in over two years. So our out-of-the-money purchase is out of the range of the market, not only for two to three months but for more than one year. The trend is up, fundamentals might have looked good, but the market doesn't have the historical range to say 76 is a great target.

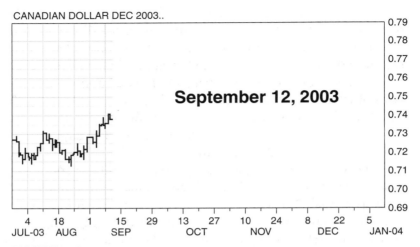

CANADIAN DOLLAR DEC 2003..

September 12, 2003

FIGURE 5-2
December Canadian chart

CANADIAN DOLLAR

FIGURE 5-3
December Canadian chart

Yet, we have the delta issue, upward trend, good market prospects, better delta. What could go wrong? The big answer—time decay. The period of 82 days is not much time for multiple option strategies to pay off. Let's take a look at how this works out and what would have been the most advantageous position in the long run. Going back to the chart, we have a really nice upward

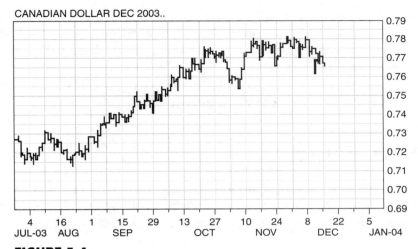

CANADIAN DOLLAR DEC 2003..

FIGURE 5-4
December Canadian chart

trend which looks to be very profitable at expiration. Let's look at the details in Figure 5-4.

The market ended trading on Dec 5, 2003, at 76.56. Holding the options till expiration would have netted a profit on both positions, but which one was better?

The at-the-money 7300 call was purchased for 1.20. The close was at 76.56. So, we subtract the total cost 74.20 (7300 + 120) from the 76.56 and we get a net gain of 2.46 or $2460 (minus cost of trading).

The four 7600 calls were purchased for 0.33, so we can take the 7633 (7600 + 33) from the 7656 = 0.23 or $230 times 4 = 92 or $920 (minus cost of trading).

The advantage is clearly to the single option purchase, even when the market went straight up over only 82 days. There was a point prior to expiration where the underlying futures reached just above 77. So, let's quickly look at the highest close the market had which was on November 28, 2003, at 77.03. Assuming the options had little or no time value because of the short time to expiration, we'll look only at the intrinsic value. Implied volatility is low, so if any time value existed at this point, it would have been minimal.

Assuming an offset of the 7300 call with the underlying futures at 77.03 capturing a premium of 4.03 in comparison offsetting sales of the 7600 calls at 1.03 each. (Remember we paid 1.20 for the 7300 and 0.33 per option on the 7600.)

7300 call   4.03 − 1.20 = 2.83 or $2830 profit minus trading costs

7600 calls   1.03 − 0.33 = 0.70 or $700 times 4 options or $2800 (minus trading costs)

The advantage is still to the single purchased option, and remember, you have four trading costs on the 7600 calls and only one on the 7300. If trading costs were equivalent to $50 per contract, the profit for the 7300 call would be even more substantial.

Remember, the major risk factors to buying options, especially out-of-the-money options, are time value and decreasing volatility.

Multiple Option Advantage

Where does a multiple option strategy have its advantages? Above we have shown a trade which was a successful position and demonstrated how the single at-the-money purchase benefited more than the multiple options over time.

The first problem with the position above is time value. There were only 82 days remaining till expiration, which leaves little time for an option to gain in value versus the continuous time value decay.

Second, the multiple options purchased were well outside of the traditional range for the market. As you'll find out more in later in the discussion on option forecasting, options that are on the outside edge of a market's recent trading range rarely gain the value they should. The very fact that time is working against the market's ability to reach to abnormal levels decreases the value traders apply to any particular contract. Professional option sellers look for these types of options for continuous premium in their portfolios.

Third, multiple option strategies such as this are often better suited for markets that may have a large volatility spike at some point. Indices and financials often run a little more steadily and at typically lower implied volatility levels than agriculture, metals, or energy. A spike higher in implied volatility will likely place additional risk value into the option increasing its time value and therefore premium. Multiple option strategies should be placed in high volatility markets at a time when the current implied volatility may be low: for example, buying spring and summer call positions for grains in the late winter. Typically volatility is lower in the winter than spring or summer. Again you have to look at the range of the market and determine if the premium you are paying plus the strike price falls into the range the market is likely to trade.

Some would argue that before expiration, the options had value and the four calls might have gained over the single call at some point. This may be true, but in the above example the market climbed at a steady rate and only peaked in the last two weeks or so of the option's life. There may have been some time value in the multiple options, but the intrinsic value plus time value and high delta of the 7300 call option would still have likely been equal to or greater than the combination of the 7600.

This is not a firm rule, high volatility markets can pay off, but on a consistent basis investing closer to the money is a better bet.

TEST YOUR KNOWLEDGE 5-1

1. Multiple option strategies are best suited for markets with low volatility. True or False?

2. A market with the potential for increasing volatility increases your risk of loss. True or False?

3. Time value is a major risk factor to buying out-of-the-money options. True or False?

CALENDAR SPREADS

When applying a calendar spread, you are simply applying option positions in a spread, within the same contract, but in differ expiration months. Many of the common spread strategies can be applied to a calendar spread, but we'll focus on some of the more common styles.

Calendar spreads are simple to understand; the calculations are identical to the related spread strategies we've already reviewed. So, rather than focus on the calculations, we'll focus on the risks and rewards.

Calendar spreads are most often used in bull call, or bear put spreads, but really can be used in most any spread format. Remember we're using the same underlying futures, only options in different expiration months. Let's work through an example.

It's September and the corn market looks good for the long term, but short term the market looks relatively stagnant or even a little lower because of harvest. The underlying futures right now are about 220 for December and 230 for March.

If the March corn 230 call is trading for around 14 and the Dec corn 230 call is trading for around 7, we might be able to offset the time value decay between now and December expiration by selling the December 230 call option and buying the March 230 call option. This would be a calendar bull call spread.

Let's look at how this works out. The December option only has about 60 days left to expiring in late November, expiring as all grain options do on the third Friday of the month prior to the underlying futures. So time decay for the December 230 call will be advanced. Time decay will move more slowly for the March 230 call. At expiration, the Dec 230 call would have zero time value and the premium would be applied to the account toward the previous purchase of the March 230 call. So the overall cost of the March 230 would be reduced to 7 (14 − 7) plus applicable trading costs on both options.

Before we go any further we need to define basis. In this instance *basis* is defined as the price difference between a futures contract in one month and a futures contract in another month. In the example above the basis between the March corn and December corn is 10 cents, March over December. In corn trading, this difference is often because of interest, carrying charges, or storage.

On the surface this sounds great, money in the bank. However, there are some risks to calendar spreads that need to be carefully analyzed before you apply calendar spreads.

First there is basis and delta. There could be a price shift because of supply, news, or other fundamental changes that would decrease or even invert the basis between the two contracts. If the December futures were to increase against the March futures or even exceed the March futures price, the result would be a change in the delta relationship between the two options. In the example above the March call is at the money and has a greater delta then the December option which is slightly out of the money. If the delta of the December option were to increase over the March option, the result would be the short December option increasing in value over the March, creating a loss. Typically, these basis shifts are slow but can be rapid if fundamentals change dramatically.

Next there is the volatility risk. If some short-term fundamental creates demand in the short December option thereby increasing implied volatility, the December option increases in value versus the March and creates a loss as well.

Finally, option expiration is the largest and most significant risk. As the market approaches expiration, if the Dec 230 call is in the money, the delta will approach 100% and be exercised into the underlying futures contract, while the March option will have a slightly lesser delta than a full futures contract. At this point the risk is in the exit of the December futures without jeopardizing the premium captured. In calendar spreads it is best to exit prior to or immediately at option expiration to avoid this risk. Once the time value is eliminated, the benefit of the option is exhausted.

Calendars and Credits

Another popular method of using calendar spreads is in a credit spread format. If we reverse the philosophy of the bull call spread above we can demonstrate how a credit spread might be used. This is not the best case scenario for a credit spread, but the example is still valid.

By reversing the above we would achieve a credit of 7 cents by selling the March 230 call and buying the December 230 call. The basis risk would apply here as well, only in the opposite format. The Dec 230 call would act as coverage for the short 230 call position. Once expiration of the Dec 230 call occurred, there would no longer be protection on the position if the Dec was out of the money. If it was in the money, the option would be exercised into the underlying December futures position and offset the delta of the March option to prevent loss from the market moving higher. Remember that only 7 cents premium was achieved so the breakeven on the December futures would be 223 (230 − 7). This position has the potential however to gain should the market rise after expiration because the December futures will outpace the March option for a short distance.

This trade is complicated and for advanced traders in specific situations and only for those traders very familiar with risk management.

Calendars can also be used in ratio spread situations such as buying one March 230 call and selling two December 250 calls. Or even in a butterfly—buying one March 230 call selling two December 250 calls, and buying one March 270 call.

Remember, when using calendar spreads, to monitor basis risk and expiration carefully. These are not "set and forget" positions.

VOLATILITY ANALYSIS—MARKET WEIGHT

Successful option trading depends on managing several factors affecting your option position. One of the factors we've touched on several times is implied volatility. To expand on our discussion of implied volatility from Chapter 2, we know that implied volatility is a measure of supply and demand for an option. The level of implied volatility varies from market to market, and we need to know how to utilize this information in option trading.

For this section we'll provide the information on implied volatility, but for your own trading you'll want to obtain an option calculator. There are many good choices for option calculators on the Web, many are free or at low cost and are typically a small software download. You'll also need historical volatility information, but that is available widely on the Web from most all data providers. If you're using a full-service broker, they'll have most all the information you need for volatility and historical volatility.

In previous chapters we've talked about the risk of volatility increasing or decreasing as a risk to option positions. We've also talked about how volatility analysis shows demand for options and market direction or at least market weight. In the example in Figure 5-5 we show two markets which have different volatility scenarios that might show market weight.

Figure 5-5 shows the December hog contract. On the call side we show implied volatility decreasing from the in-the-money strike prices to the out-of-the-money strike prices. The decreasing volatility shows that option demand is decreasing slightly as the price moves higher: a possible indication that the market's upside range is limited. Look at your futures chart to see if the technical aspect might agree with a limited upside. This could also be an indication of option sellers attempting covered call positions in the futures.

The put side of the market shows increasing volatility as the strike prices move away from the money. It's slight but could be an indication of demand in the out-of-the-money options. This could mean that outright bearish positions are being placed or long futures traders could be hedging downside risk with put options. With both indicators being on the bearish side, it might clue you in to at least a near-term market direction or market weight.

The soybean example in Figure 5-6 shows the reverse of the hog graphic. Here we have increasing volatility on the call side and decreasing volatility on the put side. This market appears to be weighted to the call side and may be looking a little bullish on this graphic. Check with your futures chart for trends and support and resistance.

With this graphic we can also look at a couple other items in volatility analysis. The historical implied volatility for soybeans ranges from around 18% to 50%, although it can stretch out of these ranges from time to time. Summer often brings higher implied volatility levels than a winter contract, but we can still look at this market as currently relatively low. You can get historical

Option	Price	Imp. Vol.	Delta	
LHZ3	54.925	0.1500	12/12/03	71 5.00%
Dec 52.000C	4.800	0.3376	0.6643	
Dec 53.000C	4.175	0.3332	0.6181	
Dec 54.000C	3.575	0.3265	0.5698	
Dec 55.000C	3.000	0.3174	0.5189	
Dec 56.000C	2.600	0.3214	0.4692	
Dec 57.000C	2.100	0.3096	0.4154	
Dec 58.000C	1.550	0.2863	0.3529	
Dec 59.000C	1.350	0.2963	0.3117	
Dec 60.000C	1.000	0.2831	0.2569	
Dec 61.000C	0.900	0.2970	0.2288	
Dec 62.000C	0.725	0.2970	0.1931	
Dec 48.000P	0.850	0.3538	−0.1715	
Dec 49.000P	1.050	0.3489	−0.2045	
Dec 50.000P	1.275	0.3427	−0.2405	
Dec 51.000P	1.575	0.3411	−0.2822	
Dec 52.000P	1.875	0.3344	−0.3250	
Dec 53.000P	2.250	0.3312	−0.3719	
Dec 54.000P	2.650	0.3255	−0.4205	
Dec 55.000P	3.075	0.3174	−0.4714	
Dec 56.000P	3.675	0.3225	−0.5209	
Dec 57.000P	4.175	0.3178	−0.5740	
Dec 58.000P	4.625	0.2896	−0.6353	

Decreasing Volatility

Increasing Volatility

FIGURE 5-5
December lean hogs

implied information off the Web or from your broker to help you with this analysis. So not only does the market lean to the bullish side on our market weight analysis, but current volatility levels appear to be low. Low implied volatility levels, as you'll remember from our call buying discussions, are usually a sign that an option may be fairly valued or even undervalued and a possible opportunity for a bullish position

The British pound example in Figure 5-7 shows increasing volatility on both sides of the market. This pattern of volatility shows a market that is building premium and demand on both sides. This is typically a sign that the market has become range bound but has potential for a significant two-sided trade. Maybe

SF4	690	0.1500	12/26/03	85	5.00%

Option	Price	Imp. Vol.	Delta
Jan 6600C	48 1/2	0.2452	0.6604
Jan 6700C	**Increasing Volatility**		0.6101
Jan 6800C	38	0.2520	0.5651
Jan 6900C	-----	-----	0.5188
Jan 7000C	29	0.2551	0.4724
Jan 7100C	-----	-----	0.4287
Jan 7200C	22	0.2599	0.3865
Jan 7300C	-----	-----	0.3443
Jan 7400C	16 3/4	0.2665	0.3121
Jan 7500C	-----	-----	0.2689
Jan 7600C	12 1/2	▼ 0.2710	0.2474
Jan 6200P	6 3/4	0.2345	–0.1564
Jan 6300P	-----	▲ -----	–0.2023
Jan 6400P	11 3/4	0.2393	–0.2364
Jan 6500P	-----	-----	–0.2837
Jan 6600P	18 1/2	0.2423	–0.3267
Jan 6700P	-----	-----	–0.3750
Jan 6800P	28	0.2511	–0.4232
Jan 6900P	-----	-----	–0.4708
Jan 7000P	40A	0.2636	–0.5137
Jan 7100P	**Decreasing Volatility**		–0.5653
Jan 7200P	-----	-----	–0.6103

FIGURE 5-6
January soybeans

a report is upcoming or a policy decision is near and traders are hedging positions on both sides depending on their vested interest. There are a number of causes, but it's important to note this in your futures analysis of the market. The market could be volatile in the near future.

This type of situation demands a look at short strangle positions. Although volatility is indicated in the future, the market is currently displaying higher implied volatility on both sides, and with only 64 days left, the time value decay may be an excellent short market opportunity. Remember your risk profile on short options and short strangles.

If this picture is reversed with volatility decreasing on each side of the market or low on each side of the market, a long strangle or straddle might be indicated

BPZ3	1.6588	0.1500	12/5/03	64	5.00%

Option	Price	Imp. Vol.	Delta
Dec 1.6300C	4.32	0.0974	0.6677
Dec 1.6400C		Increasing Volatility 0.0969	0.6115
Dec 1.6500C	3.16	0.0986	0.5545
Dec 1.6600C	2.64	0.0982	0.4968
Dec 1.6700C	2.18	0.0979	0.4390
Dec 1.6800C	1.84	0.1000	0.3855
Dec 1.6900C	1.50	0.1002	0.3331
Dec 1.7000C	1.24	0.1016	0.2868
Dec 1.7100C	1.00	0.1021	0.2430
Dec 1.7200C	0.80	0.1026	0.2037
Dec 1.5600P	0.24	0.1031	−0.0737
Dec 1.5700P	0.30	0.1004	−0.0909
Dec 1.5800P	0.40	0.0995	−0.1162
Dec 1.5900P	0.50	0.0969	−0.1423
Dec 1.6000P	0.68	0.0974	−0.1811
Dec 1.6100P	0.88	0.0967	−0.2225
Dec 1.6200P		Increasing Volatility	0.2705
Dec 1.6300P	1.44	0.0964	−0.3220

FIGURE 5-7
December British pound

to take advantage of a market breakout in the future. Just remember that such a position would need to be placed in a longer-term position. Long options are not indicated in a 60-day situation unless there are significant market indications demanding a near term move such as a report, news, or other fundamental market change.

Remember that volatility is a tool in your options arsenal, not an all-inclusive indicator. Remember also to trade within your risk profile regardless of market indications.

OPTION FORECASTING

For those who may not have a computer or access to an option calculator there are some secrets professional option traders use to forecast the value of options on the fly without tools or equipment. Traders, especially floor traders are often in quick decision situations and have to calculate an options value and delta in seconds. How do they do it? We'll show you, no tools necessary.

An option calculator will give you accurate theoretical option and future option values based on mathematical calculations of futures price, premium, volatility, and time. You can accomplish a similar calculation with your quote page. Let's take a simple option quote page like one you would find on any Web site or in the newspaper.

The option table in Figure 5-8 shows the March soybean futures and full option quotes. You'll notice we did not utilize an analysis page, just the quotes. The left column is puts, the right calls. Let's look at the January 680 call, we can see a settlement price or premium of 18.00 or 18 points. If we wanted to purchase

Open		High		Low		Last		Prev		Expiry Date		
595		601		593 1/2		596		597 1/4				

Strike	Bid	Ask	Put Last/Settle	Change	Volume	Open Int	Bid	Ask	Call Last/Settle	Change	Volume	Open Int
	-	-	-	-	-	-	-	-	-	-	-	-
3000	-	-	-	-	-	-	0.000	0.000	297.250	−29.250	32	9
3200	-	-	-	-	-	-	0.000	0.000	0.000	0.000	0	0
4000	0.000	-	0.000	0.000	0	0	0.000	0.000	0.000	0.000	0	0
4200	0.000	-	0.000	0.000	0	0	0.000	0.000	0.000	0.000	0	0
4400	0.000	-	0.000	0.000	0	0	0.000	0.000	0.000	0.000	0	0
4600	0.000	-	2.250	−0.250	2	6	0.000	0.000	0.000	0.000	0	0
4800	0.000	-	5.000	0.250	8	431	0.000	0.000	188.500	9.500	16	0
5000	0.000	-	6.500	−1.000	65	2289	0.000	0.000	0.000	0.000	0	0
5200	0.000	-	9.500	−1.750	22	608	0.000	0.000	0.000	0.000	0	0
5400	0.000	-	15.500	−0.750	31	183	0.000	0.000	0.000	0.000	0	0
5600	0.000	-	22.250	−1.250	168	980	0.000	0.000	88.000	0.000	20	191
5800	0.000	-	31.250	−0.750	462	2938	0.000	50.000	51.250	−22.500	1	654
6000	0.000	-	42.000	−1.000	53	1268	0.000	0.000	38.500	−1.500	261	282
6200	0.000	-	49.000	2.250	25	428	0.000	0.000	31.000	−1.500	3	256
6400	0.000	-	69.250	−2.000	2	210	0.000	0.000	25.000	−1.750	4	298
6600	0.000	-	0.000	0.000	0	0	0.000	0.000	20.000	−1.750	1	251
6800	0.000	-	76.000	−4.000	4	145	0.000	0.000	18.000	0.250	232	514
7000	0.000	-	138.000	5.250	1	292	0.000	0.000	14.000	−0.500	40	1472
7200	0.000	-	98.000	9.000	5	396	10.250	0.000	12.000	−1.500	18	321
7400	0.000	-	176.000	7.000	2	600	0.000	0.000	8.500	−1.500	11	809
7600	0.000	-	70.000	−11.000	0	535	0.000	7.500	8.000	−0.250	2	37
7800	0.000	-	93.000	0.000	0	100	0.000	0.000	6.500	−0.500	6	30
8000	0.000	-	0.000	0.000	0	0	0.000	5.750	6.000	−1.000	11	415
8200	0.000	-	0.000	0.000	0	0	0.000	0.000	5.250	−0.750	3	18

FIGURE 5-8
March soybean options

this option, and wanted to know what the option might be worth if the under-lying futures market fell 20 cents within a week or so of purchase, we can find out right on this page.

If the underlying futures price drops 20 cents, then the option would be 20 cents farther out of the money. So we look at the option 20 cents farther out of the money on this quote page. The 700 call is quoted at 14.00; so it makes sense that as long as no significant changes in volatility or time have occurred, a 20-cent drop in underlying futures price would equate to around 4 or 5 cents.

This gives us even more information. We now have something of an idea of the delta of the option! How? We know that a 20-cent drop moved the options value 4 cents; so if we divide 4 by 20, we have value of 0.2 or 20% delta on the March 680 option. A quick plug into the option calculator just to check shows a 20.5% delta.

What if the market rose 40 cents within a short period. First we find that the value of the 640 call is at 25 and the 680 is at 18, so the difference is 7. Therefore, a 40-cent move might make the value around 25. However, the delta will have increased a bit in this change of 40 cents so we should look at the delta of the 640 call and average the two. The delta of the 640 call is 30% and the 680 is 20%; therefore, average delta would be 25%. A 40-cent move with an average delta of 25% would be 10 cents added to the 18, or 28 cents premium. The 640 is currently at 25, so we have a good idea the premium would be between 25 and 28. The option calculator says 27.5 so we're right in the neigh-borhood with a quick mental calculation.

Remember this is all assuming little time or volatility change. So the move would have to happen within a couple of weeks or so for these values to be completely accurate, and keep in mind that this is a quick mental method and is not always 100% accurate. Some markets can be off because of volatility or limited strike prices. We recommend an option calculator or software when you have the ability.

FORECASTING WITH TIME VALUE DECAY

What happens to the options value when time starts to pass and a major market move happens later in the option's life? How would we find a reasonable guess of option premium value if a few months have passed since we applied the option trade? The best choice is to grab another quote page from an earlier expiration month and look for premium values there. The January contract

Open		High		Low		Last		Prev		Expiry Date		
588 1/2		594		586 1/2		588 1/2		590 1/2				

Strike	Bid	Ask	Last/Settle	Put Change	Volume	Open Int	Bid	Ask	Call Last/Settle	Change	Volume	Open Int
	-	-	-	-	-	-			-	-	-	-
3000	-	-	-	-	-	-	0.000	0.000	290.500	-0.500	36	3
3200	-	-	-	-	-	-	0.000	0.000	0.000	0.000	0	0
4000	0.000	-	0.000	0.000	0	0	0.000	0.000	0.000	0.000	0	0
4200	0.000	-	0.000	0.000	0	0	0.000	0.000	0.000	0.000	0	0
4400	0.000	-	0.000	0.000	0	0	0.000	0.000	0.000	0.000	0	0
4600	0.000	-	2.000	1.500	1	3	0.000	0.000	0.000	0.000	0	0
4800	0.000	-	2.500	0.000	6	542	0.000	0.000	88.000	-9.750	76	15
5000	0.000	-	4.000	-0.500	56	3590	0.000	0.000	0.000	0.000	0	0
5200	0.000	-	7.500	-0.250	89	463	0.000	0.000	120.500	-9.000	20	100
5400	0.000	-	13.000	0.250	30	2229	0.000	0.000	43.500	0.000	200	200
5600	0.000	-	19.500	-0.250	67	2033	0.000	0.000	49.500	-2.750	1	218
5800	0.000	-	28.000	-1.000	52	1714	36.750	0.000	36.500	-3.000	26	865
6000	0.000	-	40.500	0.250	23	2568	0.000	0.000	29.000	-1.500	180	2114
6200	0.000	-	43.250	6.250	56	1174	0.000	22.500	23.000	-0.500	22	1602
6400	0.000	-	67.500	-2.000	204	327	0.000	0.000	16.500	-1.500	51	1519
6600	0.000	-	84.000	1.000	18	221	0.000	0.000	13.000	-1.000	55	1301
6800	0.000	-	99.500	-1.875	5	735	0.000	0.000	9.000	-1.750	233	1230
7000	0.000	-	55.000	-23.000	0	91	0.000	0.000	7.250	-0.750	97	3059
7200	0.000	-	136.250	1.250	2	4	0.000	0.000	6.000	-0.250	43	463
7400	0.000	-	113.000	2.000	5	261	0.000	4.750	4.625	-0.375	13	552
7600	0.000	-	162.000	12.250	2	50	0.000	0.000	3.750	-0.500	22	576
7800	0.000	-	84.500	0.000	0	5	0.000	0.000	3.000	-0.500	5	142
8000	0.000	-	00.000	0.000	0	0	0.000	0.000	2.250	-0.500	88	1766

FIGURE 5-9
January soybean options

options in Figure 5-9 might show us the premium with three months' time decay. We'll have to manage any futures basis between the contracts, but remember we're looking for estimates, not figures chiseled in stone.

The January market closed at 588 ½, while the March market, in Figure 5-8, closed at 596; so the basis between the contracts is 7 ½. It's not a terribly large basis, but we might need to account for the difference in the premium estimates.

First off, if the market was to just strictly not move and time decay was the only factor, we can look a the option roughly the same distance away. This would be the 680 call. You can see the value is only 9. Almost half the time value is gone from the 18-cent value in the 680 call for March. This is an extreme decay and could be partly the responsibility of a variance in volatility and the slight basis between contracts, but it's a very strong demonstration of time value decay. You can even look at the 660 call and see that the value of 13 is less than the March option and closer to the market.

As for estimating value, it's just like our previous example. Let's say the March market has moved up 60 cents three months after applying the trade. Let's look for the January option with the same movement. If we go off the 680 call and say the market has risen 60 cents, we would need to use the January 620 call. The premium on this option is 23 cents, a profit of 5 cents over our 18-cent purchase price (minus trading costs). The value might be a touch higher because of the basis difference of 7 cents, so maybe add a penny or so. If volatility was to rise because of a fundamental change then the value could be significantly higher, but we need to work with certain constants. If the volatility was significantly lower, then it's likely the premium would be significantly lower. The options represented are at average volatility.

You can use this method to forecast value for almost any option, just don't assume it's an absolute. This is theoretical forecasting to help you decide your risk management strategy and how much time you'll allow to lapse before exiting your position if the appropriate market move is not realized.

Grab a few quote pages and practice your calculations. Remember to average in areas where there may not be a strike price represented for the change in time or value.

COMBINATIONS OF FUTURES AND OPTIONS

Using futures and options together can be one of the most effective trading methods to capitalize on short-term or long-term market action. When you trade options the ability to react to changing market price is limited to the delta of the option versus the underlying futures contract. Especially when buying options or option spreads, this delta can be frustrating when you see the underlying futures move several percent and the option position requires a significantly larger move to create the same value.

The benefits of option trading we've discussed at length, but this is one of the significant downsides to option trading and especially purchasing options. Futures trading also has many downsides because there are so few methods of limiting risk and dealing with the daily or at least short-term volatility of any market. Futures can often move very quickly, sometimes even within a particular day or session. These moves can be devastating to traders with a limited risk profile or those who have little tolerance for margin calls.

One method of limiting risk on futures is using a stop order. A *stop order* tells the broker on the floor that if the price of the underlying futures reaches a certain point the broker is to execute your offsetting position at the market. Let me give you an example.

If your purchased a December Treasury bond futures at 112.02 and only want to risk $2000 on the trade, you would need to protect the position using a stop order at 111.02 (30-year Treasury bonds are $1000 for a full point). You could then give your broker an order for 110.02 stop to sell 1 December Treasury bond. The floor broker then knows if the market is bid at 110.02 at any point, he or she is to sell one for you at the market.

You have several risks when it comes to using stop orders. Because it's a market order, in fast market conditions the order could be filled several points below where your price is. This is referred to in the industry as *slippage*. If the market moves down very quickly you could lose substantially more than your $2000 risk point even with the stop.

Another risk is that the market could open beyond your stop point. If a major fundamental market event occurred like a report, the Treasury or any market can suddenly be bid well below your stop price before it opens. This means that the broker on the floor would be executing your order at the market as soon as the first few bids fall in, but the price could again be substantially lower than where you placed your stop order.

This risk stop often leads to major frustration when a stop order, based on a short-term technical indicator or a financial-based point, is executed on nothing more than a quick market move, not a major change in trend. Traders sometimes experience being stopped out only to watch the market once again resume the trend and direction they were originally hoping for. Smaller traders with lower risk profiles can often experience this because they cannot sustain the same depth of market trade that larger traders or fund traders may be able to manage.

This is a risk of any trading in futures or stocks. The market can move very quickly and accelerate gains or losses. The risk potential of trading is also the gain potential. The market moves in a direction and gains or losses are made, which is why futures and individual stocks are traded in larger volume than options.

Options can be utilized to change the risk profile of trading futures. The limited risk advantage of buying options and premium benefit of selling options can be applied against your futures, decreasing the risk of futures volatility or even eliminating the need for a stop order and creating a bottom line to your futures trade.

We know from the discussion on buying options that a purchased option gives you the right to the underlying futures at a particular price and point in time. Since the option is the right to execute the futures at a particular price, it can be used as a protection point for a futures position in the opposite direction. By using an option you now have a right to a futures offsetting the one you currently have. We'll use the example in Figure 5-10.

In Figure 5-10 we show the Treasury futures at 112 ²⁄₃₂ or 112.02 depending on the quote system. As in our previous example if we buy the Treasury bonds at 112.02 and want to risk only $2000 or so, we can use a stop and take the risks involved with stops or we can purchase an option to give us the right

Symbol	Price	Vlty	XDate	XDays	IRate
USZ3	112 2/32	0.1500	11/21/03	50	5.00%

Option	Price	Imp. Vol.	Delta	
Dec 10900C	4 17/64	0.1512	0.6948	
Dec 11000C	3 37/64	0.1485	0.6383	
Dec 11100C	2 61/64	0.1461	0.5766	
Dec 11200C	2 25/64	0.1436	0.5113	
Dec 11300C	1 59/64	0.1429	0.4448	
Dec 11400C	1 33/64	0.1420	0.3795	
Dec 11500C	1 11/64	0.1410	0.3172	
Dec 11600C	58/64	0.1414	0.2614	
Dec 11700C	43/64	0.1402	0.2091	
Dec 11800C	32/64	0.1404	0.1654	
Dec 11900C	23/64	0.1397	0.1271	
Dec 10500P	28/64	0.1599	−0.1285	
Dec 10600P	37/64	0.1580	−0.1623	
Dec 10700P	48/64	0.1557	−0.2016	
Dec 10800P	61/64	0.1526	−0.2460	
Dec 10900P	1 13/64	0.1497	−0.2968	
Dec 11000P	1 33/64	0.1476	−0.3542	
Dec 11100P	1 57/64	0.1456	−0.4164	
Dec 11200P	2 21/64	0.1436	−0.4819	
Dec 11300P	2 55/64	0.1433	−0.5482	
Dec 11400P	3 29/64	0.1429	−0.6128	
Dec 11500P	4 7/64	0.1424	−0.6742	

FIGURE 5-10
December treasury bonds

to offset the position. A put option would give us the right to sell the underlying futures, which would be an offset to the long position applied at 112.02.

In Figure 5-10 we can see that the highlighted premium of the 112 put option is 221/64. (Treasury options are in 64ths rather than the 32ds of futures.) By purchasing this option we now have the right to the underlying futures at 112. We have purchased the futures at 112.02 and the right to sell the futures at 112. So the risk, or basis between the futures purchase and the put purchase, must be accounted for in the total risk analysis of the trade: 112.02 − 112.00 = 0.02 or $\frac{2}{32}$, which in treasury bonds equals $62.50 ($1000/32 = $31.25 × 2 = $62.50).

In addition, we have to add the premium spent on the option position plus costs of trading to the total risk of the position. The 112 put shows a cost of 2 $\frac{21}{64}$ or $2328.12 (two full points = $2000 + 21 × $15.625 = $2328.12). Then we need to add the difference between options and futures of $62.50 + $2328.12 = $2390.62 plus costs of trading on the future and option position.

The risk of utilizing the at-the-money option here is a bit higher than the $2000 we were looking for, but remember the risk is entirely fixed. The only potential risk beyond the numbers is margin risk. Because an option builds or loses value at a rate slower than the underlying futures, you could be responsible for margin funds to cover the future until you exercise the option. The cash value of the option is not available typically until you sell the option position, although the initial margin charged on the futures position will be typically less.

Let's take a quick look at the P&L for this type of trade. The maximum risk we know is 2390.62. To find out where the position is profitable if we were to allow the option to expire, we must add the premium to the futures price just as in a purchased option calculation. The premium roughly translates to 2 $\frac{11}{32}$, meaning the ultimate breakeven would be 114 $\frac{13}{32}$ (2 $\frac{11}{32}$ + 112 $\frac{2}{32}$) plus trading costs.

We have to remember though that the ultimate purpose for this trade type is to take advantage of the movement of the underlying futures without using a risky stop or suffering from market volatility. The option in this case is a safety net. The 112 put option is the at-the-money put, so it has a delta somewhere near 50%. So for each point the futures move, the option is only going to gain or lose roughly 50% in value, decreasing as the market moves upward, increasing as the market falls. So, as the market moves in your favor, your profitability increases rapidly while still having a safety net of the 112 put. If the market moves against you, the put option will increase in value making up for a percentage of the losses until the maximum risk is achieved.

It is important to remember that you may be responsible for margin on the underlying futures for losses until the option can be exercised or sold.

COVERED OPTIONS

A popular trend in trading stocks and commodities recently has been to tout the technique of using covered calls or in the case of short selling covered puts. When using covered options you are using techniques you have already learned in our discussions on selling options, but here we'll apply it to the underlying future or outright stock position. If you remember, when selling options you are selling the right and taking on the obligation to the underlying futures. Since you are long the underlying futures in our example, at some point the underlying futures will offset the obligation of the short call or covered call option. The technique is the same as a bull call spread with the exception of the enhanced delta of the underlying futures and also the unlimited risk of the underlying future. Let's look at the example in the Treasury bonds again but with the example modified and highlighted for a short call.

In Figure 5-11 we highlight selling the 116 call at a premium of $^{58}/_{64}$, and we'll continue the example of purchasing one December Treasury bond at 112.02. The 116 call's premium can be applied to the risk of the trade and help lower the breakeven of the position. With the sold premium of $^{58}/_{64}$, or $^{29}/_{32}$, we can reduce the downside breakeven to 111.05. Because it is a single call sell against a single futures contract, the obligation to sell the underlying future will offset gains in the futures contract at 116 at expiration. So the maximum profit on this position is 4 $^{29}/_{32}$ (116 + $^{29}/_{32}$) − 112 = 4 $^{29}/_{32}$ or $4906.26 minus trading costs. The maximum loss is unlimited, but loss does not begin to occur at option expiration until 111.05. Remember, you will be responsible for margin on the underlying futures contract.

Covered options can be utilized in multiple option sales against the underlying futures position as well. Remember the delta of the option is less than the underlying futures. In the case of the 116 call it's around 26%. So at current prices, four short options would roughly have the delta of one underlying futures contract. Remember though that if the market were to rise, so then would the delta of the combined options. Ratios can be very effective tools for collecting premium utilizing the futures position as coverage for the short options.

In this case, if we were to look at the chart and see a resistance point at 117 a multiple option sale of four 117 call options against the underlying futures would capture significant premium ($^{43}/_{64}$ × 4 = 1 $^{72}/_{64}$ or $^{86}/_{32}$ or 2 $^{22}/_{32}$). This would bring the futures breakeven down to 109.12 and the upside breakeven would be roughly 118 $^{7}/_{32}$ (4 $^{30}/_{32}$ ÷ 4 + 117) minus trading costs. If the market were to remain above 112.02 or even advance during the term, but remain below the 117 mark, a substantial profit could be gained on both

USZ3	112 2/32 0.1500 11/21/03		50 5.00%	
Option	**Price**	**Imp. Vol.**	**Delta**	
Dec 10900C	4 17/64	0.1512	0.6948	
Dec 11000C	3 37/64	0.1485	0.6383	
Dec 11100C	2 61/64	0.1461	0.5766	
Dec 11200C	2 25/64	0.1436	0.5113	
Dec 11300C	1 59/64	0.1429	0.4448	
Dec 11400C	1 33/64	0.1420	0.3795	
Dec 11500C	1 11/64	0.1410	0.3172	
Dec 11600C	58/64	0.1414	0.2614	
Dec 11700C	43/64	0.1402	0.2091	
Dec 11800C	32/64	0.1404	0.1654	
Dec 11900C	23/64	0.1397	0.1271	
Dec 10500P	28/64	0.1599	−0.1285	
Dec 10600P	37/64	0.1580	−0.1623	
Dec 10700P	48/64	0.1557	−0.2016	
Dec 10800P	61/64	0.1526	−0.2460	
Dec 10900P	1 13/64	0.1497	−0.2968	
Dec 11000P	1 33/64	0.1476	−0.3542	
Dec 11100P	1 57/64	0.1456	−0.4164	
Dec 11200P	2 21/64	0.1436	−0.4819	
Dec 11300P	2 55/64	0.1433	−0.5482	
Dec 11400P	3 29/64	0.1429	−0.6128	
Dec 11500P	4 7/64	0.1424	−0.6742	

FIGURE 5-11
December treasury bonds

sides of the market. However, you must remember that there is unlimited risk on both sides of this trade. The upside risk is substantial as four options would become increasingly more price and margin risk as the market rose. It's very important to have a defined risk strategy and exit point prior to entering this type of position. It is a high-risk trade.

FUTURES COVERED RISK REVERSAL

Combining covered options with the strategy of using purchased options for protecting futures positions can provide a more secure trading situation. Figure

5-12 shows an example of the risk reversal, which in this case would be buying the 112 put and selling the 116 call option. Both the purchased put and short call have short market delta, in this case around 75%.

In Figure 5-12, we have reduced the cost of the put purchase by selling the 116 call, thereby reducing the overall risk to the position to 1 ¹⁴⁄₃₂. The position now has a maximum profit potential of 2 ¹⁸⁄₃₂ or $2562.50.

This example is a very narrow spread, but it gives you an idea of how you can effectively utilize short call premium to offset the cost of the protective put position when using options to cover the underlying futures.

You should keep in mind that you will be responsible for the futures margin and losses until the options are liquidated and the premium gained from the

USZ3	112 2/32	0.1500	11/21/03	50	5.00%
Option	Price	Imp. Vol.	Delta	
Dec 10900C	4 17/64	0.1512	0.6948	
Dec 11000C	3 37/64	0.1485	0.6383	
Dec 11100C	2 61/64	0.1461	0.5766	
Dec 11200C	2 25/64	0.1436	0.5113	
Dec 11300C	1 59/64	0.1429	0.4448	
Dec 11400C	1 33/64	0.1420	0.3795	
Dec 11500C	1 11/64	0.1410	0.3172	
Dec 11600C	58/64	0.1414	0.2614	
Dec 11700C	43/64	0.1402	0.2091	
Dec 11800C	32/64	0.1404	0.1654	
Dec 11900C	23/64	0.1397	0.1271	
Dec 10500P	28/64	0.1599	−0.1285	
Dec 10600P	37/64	0.1580	−0.1623	
Dec 10700P	48/64	0.1557	−0.2016	
Dec 10800P	61/64	0.1526	−0.2460	
Dec 10900P	1 13/64	0.1497	−0.2968	
Dec 11000P	1 33/64	0.1476	−0.3542	
Dec 11100P	1 57/64	0.1456	−0.4164	
Dec 11200P	2 21/64	0.1436	−0.4819	
Dec 11300P	2 55/64	0.1433	−0.5482	
Dec 11400P	3 29/64	0.1429	−0.6128	
Dec 11500P	4 7/64	0.1424	−0.6742	

FIGURE 5-12
December treasury bonds

option is recovered. You can also combine these strategies in any format with a farther from the market put as your ultimate safety net for a futures trade or options in a number of configurations. If you are not an experienced trader, I recommend getting professional help when utilizing these positions. Risk management is the most important issue when combining futures and options or trading futures in general.

These examples use long put options, long futures, and short calls; however, the reverse can be used in short market situations using long call options, short futures, and short puts.

SYNTHETIC FUTURES

The last advanced strategy we'll discuss is a synthetic futures position. The synthetic futures position is a risk reversal spread which has been created at the same strike price. The construction and calculations are the same as the risk reversal. To give you an example, a synthetic futures position would be created if you were to sell the 580 July sugar put and buy the 580 July sugar call. The same would be true if you were selling the 580 call and buying the 580 put. The delta of the put and the call should add up to 100%, equaling one futures position.

The advantage of creating a synthetic futures position over a standard futures position is mostly for your broker, two trades rather than one, but there are instances where there may be high implied volatility on the short option creating an opportunity to capture premium. It would be common for this type of position in a high implied volatility situation to be combined with a futures position moving in the opposite direction to capitalize on time value decay, volatility, or a basis between the underlying futures position and the strike price of the options.

CHAPTER TEST

1. Which of the following represents a calendar spread?
   (a) Buying Dec British pound 170 call, selling Dec Canadian dollar 79 call
   (b) Selling Dec British pound 170 call, selling Dec British pound 160 put
   (c) Buying Dec British pound 170 call, selling March British pound 190 call
   (d) Buying Dec British pound 170 call, selling Dec British pound 190 call

2. Which of the following is a risk of buying multiple options?
   (a) Multiple trading commissions and fees
   (b) Time value decay
   (c) Decrease in implied volatility
   (d) All of the above

3. Multiple option strategies can be effective tools when
   (a) Advertised as seasonal trades
   (b) Bought at extremely low implied volatility
   (c) At-the-money options are expensive
   (d) None of the above

4. The net delta of a purchased at-the-money put and a long futures would be closest to
   (a) 49%
   (b) 100%
   (c) 38%
   (d) 79%

5. Forecasting options gives you the ability to do which of the following?
   (a) Estimate option value
   (b) Tell you absolutely where an option is going to be in three months
   (c) Determine possible delta
   (d) a and c

6. Which of the following best describes the risk of a combination of a long put, long futures, short call?
   (a) Limited risk, unlimited profit potential, high premium risk
   (b) Limited risk, limited profit potential, low premium risk

     (c) Unlimited risk, limited profit potential, premium credit

     (d) None of the above

7. Which of the following best describes the risk of a covered call spread?

     (a) Limited risk, unlimited profit potential, high premium risk.

     (b) Limited risk, limited profit potential, low premium risk

     (c) Unlimited risk, limited profit potential, premium credit

     (d) None of the above

8. Which of the following best describes the risk of covered put options?

     (a) Limited risk, unlimited profit potential, high premium risk.

     (b) Limited risk, limited profit potential, low premium risk

     (c) Unlimited risk, limited profit potential, small premium credit

     (d) Unlimited risk, limited profit potential, risk on both sides

9. A calendar spread can offer which?

     (a) Time decay on short-term options

     (b) Longer-term options purchased with some implied volatility risk offset

     (c) Short-term protection on long-term short option positions

     (d) All of the above

10. High implied volatility is a negative for which of the following?

     (a) Multiple out of the money options

     (b) Puts purchased against long futures

     (c) Long strangle

     (d) All of the above

ANSWERS TO TESTS

Test Your Knowledge 5-1

1. False. Buying multiple options in low implied volatility situations in markets that typically have high volatility is the best situation for this type of purchase. 2. False. Your maximum risk on a purchased option is premium plus trading costs. 3. True. Time value and decreasing volatility are the two major risks to any option purchase, especially out-of-the-money options

Chapter Test

1. c. Calendar spreads are options in different contract months.
2. d. All these are risks when buying multiple out-of-the-money options.
3. b. Low volatility provides the best bet for this type of strategy.
4. a. The at-the-money put should be somewhere near 50%, and the futures contract always has a delta of 100%.
5. d. Answers *a* and *c* are both correct.
6. b. This answer would be the most correct depending on conditions.
7. c. You would capture premium against the underlying futures but have unlimited downside risk and limited profit potential.
8. c. The fact that it is a put does not change the risk.
9. d. All of these can be correct when using various calendar spreads.
10. d. All of these are potential risks when buying high implied volatility.

CHAPTER 6

RISK MANAGEMENT

In Chapter 6 we will dig into the most crucial part of any investment strategy, risk management. We'll cover:

- Time value management
- Risk-management strategies
- Hedging techniques
- Option trading techniques and professional tips
- Hedging with options

TIME VALUE MANAGEMENT

As we've previously discussed, time value is one of the premier risks of purchasing options. Managing time value and time decay is essential to profitable option trading. We need to identify the risk areas of purchasing options and how to manage these risks. In Chapter 2, we discussed the basics of time value and intrinsic value of options and how time value or risk value decay as option expiration nears. On the day of expiration time value will be zero.

In general, market time value accelerates in the last 45 days of the option's life, but you can apply the following general rules to your option trading. Options greater than 100 days in time till expiration will generally have a very slow theta or rate of decay. This rate accelerates from that point. As a general rule, you can assume that an option will decay approximately 50% of the time value from inception to the last 60 days. The remaining 50% of time value is eliminated from 60 days to 0.

In further identifying the risks and strategy of time value, we need to do a little research and discover how a particular market handles time value. Each is different depending on the overall volatility of the underlying futures contract and the average implied volatility of the particular market. The best way to research a market's time value is to look at the deferred options of the market and see how much time value is remaining. Compare this to the upfront options and look to see if any substantial time value remains in the last 30 to 45 days of the options.

Track the options from 100 days (or more) and create a chart of the time value (not the actual value) of the at-the-money calls and puts. Continue your research as a part of any paper trading tracking program or as a part of your normal trading research. Do this for all the options you are interested in trading. As you begin your trading, you'll develop a baseline for time value decay. You'll end up with a chart showing time value rates of decay on the markets you like to trade. We suggest plotting the time value on the chart weekly; remember that you're just charting the at-the-money options, not a particular option or strike price.

The time value pattern can help you decide how to handle option trading for that market. Use your chart and general rules to decide where the acceleration point is and maintain option purchases beyond this point. If an option loses 30% of its value by 70 days and accelerates quickly to 45 days, buy options only 100 days and greater. When the options go through 70 days, the options should be evaluated for profitability or be moved to deferred contracts (contracts further away in time). When you are selling options, use your research to pinpoint when time value accelerates (usually 60 days or less) to sell option premium.

Long-term option premium sales or captures can be effective, but be prepared to deal with market volatility and margin until the time value accelerates.

Short-Term Purchasing

Sometimes it may seem appropriate to purchase options with short terms of 45 days or less until expiration. These options have risk of extreme time decay; however, the lack of time value can also make them attractively affordable. In most cases, this leads to losses because if the market does not move quickly enough to offset the time decay the option will expire worthless.

In the face of market reports or strong fundamental changes, it may be appropriate to use these options as long as you understand the risk of the entire option premium is necessary. There may not be time to recover any premium if the result of the fundamental event does not benefit the option position.

Short-term options can also be effective stops for futures positions because of the relatively low premium levels, just be aware again that the entire premium is at risk and should be expected to be lost.

RISK-MANAGEMENT STRATEGIES

Risk management is the most important part of any trading strategy, futures, options, stocks, or bonds. A predesigned risk-management strategy will make the difference between successful long-term trading or investing and failure.

Most frequently, risk management fails, even among professional traders, because of emotional attachment to a particular trade or market direction. It's common to hear traders say, "Oh it'll come back," or "The weather's changing," etc, etc. A book full of excuses could be written from a single day's trade in the markets. It's going to get too warm, too cold, too dry, war, peace, supply, demand.

Fundamental changes are the driving force to the market, but short term the market may not react to fundamental changes for many reasons. The events may be previously factored into the trade, financial players may have other interests in the market, funds may be already weighted to one side of the market or another. The facts are that markets sometimes respond to fundamental indications and sometimes do not. Technical indications are more reliable for short-term market support and resistance and are better for risk management. They are less subjective to individual trading and investing decisions. Risk strategies pinned to technical indications will often be more effective and reduce losses.

To avoid the emotional or subjective risks of the market, we have developed risk strategies that we recommend for consistency. The strategies are simple, but the consistent usage is usually the most difficult part of any trading strategy. We'll discuss each strategy related to futures and options trading. These strategies could be applied to stock and bonds as well.

STOP ORDERS

We've discussed some of the limitations of stop orders. They can have risk at the open of a market or during fast market conditions. However, stops are an ultimate out at some point from a market which may be moving against your position. When a stop price is executed, the order becomes a market order and will be filled on a best efforts basis at the nearest bid or offer at the current market. Slippage on stop orders is reasonable and manageable 90% of the time.

Stop orders can be utilized on futures in pretty much all markets and on options in most. A stop order on an option is created by giving your broker a premium price for the option at which the broker is to execute the offsetting order at the market in the same fashion as a futures order except with the premium as the stop out price.

Stops should be used based on monetary necessity, but preferably based on technical indications of support or resistance on the futures chart. You should use your options forecasting technique to determine where the option premium might be at the futures level indicated at the technical stop.

Stop orders are especially indicated for short options and futures. A preexisting stop order placed GTC, or good till canceled, could save hundreds or thousands of dollars on a particular trade gone wrong. If you are not available to monitor the markets, or do not have a broker monitoring the market on your behalf, you should be using stop orders. Remember that short options stops are placed on the premium price.

Stops could also be used to buy protection on open risk futures or options positions. For example, if you were long the underlying futures contract and did not want the risk of being stopped out on intraweek market volatility, you might consider using your option forecasting technique to determine the premium at which a stop order would be executed and place an order with your broker to buy the appropriate put option on a buy stop. With this method a put option would be executed to protect your underlying futures contract, as we demonstrated in the section "Combinations of Futures and Options" in Chapter 5. This strategy can help you avoid immediate premium risk and being stopped out on near-term market volatility.

A sell stop can also be used to on long option positions to protect the value of the premium of the option and further define risk of purchased options. Long-term at-the-money options can often be expensive or have high premium levels. Once again, use your option forecasting technique to determine where the premium might be at your futures support or resistance level. Place a sell stop with your broker at the premium price indicated to sell the option.

MARKET PRICE MONITORING

Professional traders often trade on instinct using a particular market price or point based on technical indicators. This is a high-risk trading strategy because no fixed risk point is in place.

Using this strategy is acceptable with purchased options because the risk is established with the total of premium invested; however short options or futures positions can have fast-moving price changes which can move beyond your risk point before you can notice the market movement.

We do not recommend price monitoring unless you have a professional broker or trader with authorization to execute offsetting trades on your behalf.

PREMIUM LEVELS

When selling option premium, or creating short neutral delta spreads such as short straddles and strangles, we recommend utilizing another method for risk management: assigning a premium level based on monetary risk.

We normally recommend double the captured premium, but those with higher risk profiles might consider triple the captured premium. This method establishes a risk point for selling options based on the theory that if the premium were to double against the position, either the volatility would be exploding or the market would have penetrated the resistance area used to consider the sale.

For example, if the corn market had an upper resistance area at 250 and you were to sell the 260 call option for 7 cents and if the premium were to double or triple against the position on a short-term option, the odds are the futures market has penetrated 250 and could be moving to a new trend.

We often recommend using a stop order with this type of strategy. If you are using a short strangle or straddle, you would take the sum of the entire captured premium and double it to find the risk point. So if you sold a 260 call for 7 and a 220 put for 7, then your stop would be located at 28. You would apply this to each option with instructions to cancel the opposing order if one gets executed.

The premium stop is an effective means of taking the subjective analysis out of the equation.

MONETARY RISK POINTS

Smaller traders often base their risk points on an amount per trade. This is a sensible risk management method based on your investment profile. An example would be "I only want to risk $1000 on this trade." *You should never risk more than you can afford to lose.* When you are trading using monetary stops, you need to change your strategy slightly. You should be looking for defined technical support and resistance areas on the chart that fit within the parameters of your monetary risk.

By doing this you place yourself in a position to capitalize on what larger traders may be doing within your limited monetary risk strategy. Make sure that when you are using a defined monetary risk, you utilize stop orders or purchased protective options to make certain your risk is defined and not subjective.

All traders should consider monetary risk on a per trade basis to extend their opportunity for success. Not every trade will be a winner, and you want to keep a certain amount of funds available for margin or other trading opportunities.

TAKING PROFITS

There is probably no better advice for market trading than "Let your winners ride and cut your losers short." But in the modern market long-term trading can be subject to significant volatility. Using risk management on winning trades is just as important as on the losers. Protecting profitability on trades leads to another old saying… "You won't go broke taking profits."

When you are protecting profits, we recommend trailing stops behind your profitable positions. Let's take an example. You purchase the June S&P 500 at 1105 on a short-term trade and the market closes at 1110 at the end of the day. If you are a futures trader, it would make sense that the market may follow through in the next session with additional gains. To protect yourself and to set yourself up for continuing profits, consider trailing a stop below where the market closed, but with a smaller loss or even a profit built into the stop. Maybe a stop at 1105.25 would be sensible for the next day's session.

With options the same is true. An option which moves into the money and has a healthy profit should be protected. Consider putting a stop on the option above the premium you paid initially. This way if the market changes direction, you may have the opportunity to recover your initial investment.

There is no crime in just setting a profit-and-loss point for each trade. In cyclical markets like the grains, trends can last for a week, a month, or six months. The difficulty is to know how to manage a one-week profit and still have a market position for the six-month trend that might develop. When trading long options, you might consider rolling profitable positions before they lose their time value. An example would be that you purchased a 340 wheat call which has doubled in premium. Sell the 340 call and reinvest your initial investment in the 360 call. You have your money back and a free position in a market.

When you make substantial profits in markets, take some home, especially in commodity trading. Take a percentage of your winning trades and remove it from your trading account. This will help prevent you from overleveraging your future investments beyond what you originally decided to risk in trading. If you are trying to build account value and investment capability, then make certain to set a percentage of excess margin that should be maintained and only leverage based on the percentages you establish. Set your rules and stick to them. It will save you money, frustration, and time.

HEDGING BASICS

Hedging is the process of protecting hard commodity pricing for producers, processors, or end users. Those with vested interests in commodity products need to protect their bottom line from the uncertainty of fluctuations in pricing for output or input of products.

The commodity futures or derivative markets were created for this purpose. When you are hedging, you are utilizing a derivative contract to offset the need of your business's bottom line. If you are a farmer and produce corn and soybeans, your concern would be what price you might be able to achieve at harvest time for your crop. A processor or miller would be concerned with the input price of raw product for processing, like soybeans processed into soy meal or soy oil.

Commodity products other than domestic agriculture are also used in hedging. Gold mining companies utilize gold futures to protect price or even sell product. Sugar, coffee, cotton, crude oil, and gasoline are all hedging products. Even the financial products are excellent tools for hedging. A mortgage company or broker might utilize Treasury bonds to lock in interest rates. An exporter might use currency contracts to lock in exchange rates ahead of a major purchase or sale. New single stock futures can even be used for hedging in the stock market along with the traditional index contracts such as the NASDAQ, e-mini NASDAQ, S&P 500, e-mini S&P, Dow Jones, and e-mini Dow.

This discussion will focus on the basis of hedging using underlying futures contracts. It is important to grasp the concept of hedging and the techniques involved before looking at options. First let's repeat our definition of basis: The basis relating to cash commodities is the variance in price between the cash price paid locally and the equivalent futures contract traded at the exchange. Let's look at some examples of using futures contracts for hedging.

Commodity Hedges

The techniques involved in hedging commodities are not much different than making trading decisions for speculative trading. Technical support and resistance levels and fundamental and technical market trends are the basic indicators for hedging decisions. Often hedge decisions are difficult because using straight futures can result in a restriction on profit potential even though they can mean a lock-in of profit or a minimization of losses.

Hedging differs from trading in this form also because it needs to be viewed from a business standpoint. The mistakes brokers and traders see made by hedgers involve treating their business decisions as trading decisions. As a hedger it's important to distinguish the business from speculation and make decisions that continue business profitability. Few businesses have the opportunity to lock in profit for their business with a simple trade or two. Hedgers should recognize this special distinction and treat hedge decisions as business decisions.

OPTION HEDGING TECHNIQUES

With the basics of futures hedging in mind we can now focus on the benefits of hedging with options. Since a purchased option gives us the right but not the obligation to the underlying futures, according to our definition of an option, this is a perfect tool for hedging.

We've discovered the benefits and downsides to purchasing options, but let's focus on the advantages for hedge purposes, keeping in mind the risks we've previously discussed.

Earlier we learned that hedgers use futures contracts to lock in price against their cash futures product or need. Since a purchased option has the same right as the futures, but not the obligation, it changes the risk to the hedger significantly. The major downside of reducing profitability can be eliminated using purchased options.

Let's look at an example of using options for hedging in Figure 6-1. A hog producer in Illinois had a pretty standard basis of $2 under the futures for delivery to the meat packer. Her breakeven on the hog is around $46/hundred

LHZ3	54.925	0.1500	12/12/03	71	5.00%

Option	Price	Imp. Vol.	Delta
Dec 52.000C	4.800	0.3376	0.6643
Dec 53.000C	4.175	0.3332	0.6181
Dec 54.000C	3.575	0.3265	0.5698
Dec 55.000C	3.000	0.3174	0.5109
Dec 56.000C	2.600	0.3214	0.4692
Dec 57.000C	2.100	0.3096	0.4154
Dec 58.000C	1.550	0.2863	0.3529
Dec 59.000C	1.350	0.2963	0.3117
Dec 60.000C	1.000	0.2831	0.2569
Dec 61.000C	0.900	0.2970	0.2288
Dec 62.000C	0.725	0.2970	0.1931
Dec 48.000P	0.850	0.3538	−0.1715
Dec 49.000P	1.050	0.3489	−0.2045
Dec 50.000P	1.275	0.3427	−0.2405
Dec 51.000P	1.575	0.3411	−0.2822
Dec 52.000P	1.875	0.3344	−0.3250
Dec 53.000P	2.250	0.3312	−0.3719
Dec 54.000P	2.650	0.3255	−0.4205
Dec 55.000P	3.075	0.3174	−0.4714
Dec 56.000P	3.675	0.3225	−0.5209
Dec 57.000P	4.175	0.3118	−0.5740
Dec 58.000P	4.625	0.2896	−0.6353

FIGURE 6-1
December lean hogs

lean weight (CME hogs are quoted in lean weight approximately 74% of live weight). So she knows that she has to get at least 48 for her hogs on the futures to break even. The outlook for hog prices appears to be positive and she doesn't want to cut off the profit potential of the hogs if they go to 60 or more. She can use an option to reduce this downside risk and even lock in a slight profit, while still leaving the market upside open.

Figure 6-1 shows the December hog futures trading at 54.92. We've highlighted the purchase of the December 55 put, which is just slightly in the money. The premium of this put option is 3.075 or $1230. Calculate the hedge effectiveness of this put option by using your technique for calculating breakeven on a purchased option:

$$55.00 - 3.07 = 51.925$$

The hedge will be effective at 51.925, locking in a floor price for the farmer at 51.925 minus basis or 49.925. The advantage comes from the upside of the market being still open after the premium of the option is covered. Remember, 3.075 was spent. We take the current futures price and add the premium of 3.07:

$$54.925 + 3.075 = 58.00$$

So, if the futures price was to rise beyond the price of 58.00 then our farmer is once again making money on the cash hogs with no limitations. Because this is a purchased option, the trading risk is limited to the premium and costs of trading, so no additional margin will be required.

Another example would be to purchase the 52 put option. This option has a little lower premium at 1.875. Let's look at the hedge effectiveness and the return to gain of this option.

$$52.00 - 1.875 = 50.125 \text{ hedge effective}$$

$$54.925 + 1.857 = 56.80 \text{ return to gain or recapture price}$$

So, the 52 put has an effective price 1.79 below the 55 put, but also returns to a gain at 56.80, which is 1.20 quicker than the 55 put.

You should calculate several options and their value to your hedge need before executing a position for your needs. Purchased options apply a limited risk, unlimited profit aspect to cash transactions.

The same would apply if you were trying to hedge these hogs for input into your packing plant. Buying the 55 call option at 3.00 would give you a maximum purchase price for December delivery hogs at 58. The packer would recapture the price of the option at 51.92

Covered Options

Producer or end users of a commodity product are technically in the futures because of their interest in the market. Producers of soybeans would be long the product because they have possession of it, just like a long futures position. Processors of soybeans would technically be short the market, because they have a continuous need to buy the product.

This gives hedgers a unique opportunity to utilize covered option positions. The soybean producer can sell call options against held crop and capture premium with the only risks being basis of cash to futures and coming up with margin for the short option when necessary. In this case selling a call option would limit the profit of that cash crop as well.

The soybean processor could sell put premium against future purchase of soybeans to capture premium. The sold put would be the obligation to purchase soybeans that need to be purchased in the future anyway. The risks again would be basis to cash and margin for the trade.

The advantage to capturing this covered premium is that with options you can choose strike prices that are advantageous for your position. In other words, it can be well out of the money to where there is a better opportunity for the option to expire out of the money and capture the entire premium to apply to the purchase or sale of the underlying cash commodity.

Window Hedges

Combining the strategies above creates a window hedge. This is one of the most effective hedging strategies you can use. The window hedge takes advantage of the bottom-line pricing of the purchased option with the captured premium of the out-of-the-money short option applied to the cost of the purchased option. Let's look at an example in Figure 6-2 of a sale of the Dec hog 60 call to clarify how this works.

This is a risk reversal from your spread lessons, but when applied in hedging, we call it a *window hedge*.

In the example of the hog farmer above we demonstrated the purchase of the 52 put at 1.875. When we apply the sale of the 60 at 1.00 call, this reduces the cost of the put option, further improving the effective price of the hedge. Let's look at the calculation:

$$1.87 - 1.00 = 0.87 \text{ total premium}$$

$$52.00 - 0.87 = 51.12 \text{ effective hedge (minus basis)}$$

$$54.92 + 0.87 = 55.80 \text{ recapture (return to gain)}$$

What this means is that the hog farmer now has a floor price at 51.12 and regains the ability to make money on the hogs at 55.80 all the way up to 59.12 (60.00 – 0.87 premium) where the obligation to sell the underlying futures would eliminate further profit potential on the hogs. The window would be 51.12 to 59.12.

On the packer side we'll see the same type trade only reversed using a short put and long call position.

LHZ3	54.925	0.1500	12/12/03	71	5.00%
Option	**Price**	**Imp. Vol.**	**Delta**		
Dec 52.000C	4.800	0.3376	0.6643		
Dec 53.000C	4.175	0.3332	0.6181		
Dec 54.000C	3.575	0.3265	0.5698		
Dec 55.000C	3.000	0.3174	0.5109		
Dec 56.000C	2.600	0.3214	0.4692		
Dec 57.000C	2.100	0.3096	0.4154		
Dec 58.000C	1.550	0.2863	0.3529		
Dec 59.000C	1.350	0.2963	0.3117		
Dec 60.000C	1.000	0.2831	0.2569		
Dec 61.000C	0.900	0.2970	0.2288		
Dec 62.000C	0.725	0.2970	0.1931		
Dec 48.000P	0.850	0.3538	−0.1715		
Dec 49.000P	1.050	0.3489	−0.2045		
Dec 50.000P	1.275	0.3427	−0.2405		
Dec 51.000P	1.575	0.3411	−0.2822		
Dec 52.000P	1.875	0.3344	−0.3250		
Dec 53.000P	2.250	0.3312	−0.3719		
Dec 54.000P	2.650	0.3255	−0.4205		
Dec 55.000P	3.075	0.3174	−0.4714		
Dec 56.000P	3.675	0.3225	−0.5209		
Dec 57.000P	4.175	0.3118	−0.5740		
Dec 58.000P	4.625	0.2896	−0.6353		

FIGURE 6-2
December lean hogs

Remember that these hedge trade positions require sensible trading deci-sions as much as speculative trades. You should follow the rules you've learned on trading volatility and time value. Just because it's a hedge, it doesn't neces-sarily change the rules regarding short-term option positions or trading implied volatility. Only if it's a necessary business decision should you break the rules we've discussed for trading options in general.

Options can be used in other formats for specialized hedging needs. For example, a cattle operation might purchase cattle in August and sell them in April. The cattle operation might consider buying feeder cattle calls to protect the August purchase prices, and then purchase the live cattle puts in April to protect the sale price of cattle. Windows could be used in this situation as well as selling puts and buying calls for the feeder cattle side and selling calls and buying puts on the live cattle side

Crude oil is another market where you have products from a single commodity. In crude it's referred to as *crack spreads* from the process of "cracking" products from the raw crude oil. So, as a hedger in this market you would be interested in covering the input prices of crude and output of products. Options can be effective tools for hedging in this situation just like the cattle above.

Always keep in mind the risks we've discussed with trading options, time value decay, implied volatility, and basis when making trading decisions. Also keep in mind the effectiveness of using options to protect your bottom line and leave your product upside open. Options make a fantastic addition to your hedging and trading arsenal.

Cash Replacement

Cash replacement is a hedge strategy that is arguably speculative in nature, but we should briefly cover the basics of the philosophy. Cash replacement is best served with purchased options or limited risk option spreads.

The theory of cash replacement is when a producer or someone with a vested interest in a particular commodity contracts for purchase or sale of the cash commodity and wants to re-own that commodity in the futures market. The purpose would be to regain the profit potential of the commodity without the risk of holding the cash product any longer. Because it is related to product already price locked by contract, we do not want to re-own the risk of the cash commodity.

A couple of quick examples: A silver mining company makes a large sale of silver to cover operating expenses at a market cycle low on the chart. To regain some of the potential from the silver they just sold, they might consider buying some long-term call options or bull call spreads to take advantage of a market rebound without the risk of losing anything above the premium and trading costs.

Cash replacement is often an aftereffect of improper hedging in the first place, but it can be an effective tool for regaining profit on cash positions. Remember when you are cash replacing to consider the risk of spending the premium, the time value decay, and the implied volatility.

OPTION TRADING TIPS

As we wrap up your option education we want to give you some tips and tricks for successful option trading.

1. **Limit Orders** When entering option positions avoid using market orders. Market orders give the broker on the floor discretion to fill your order at the best price available at the time. However, the spread between bid and offer can be wide, especially in markets with less volume.

2. **VOI** Watch the *v*olume and *o*pen *i*nterest of the individual option strike price you might be interested in. This is an important tool when trading options. If the option has low volume and especially low open interest, it could be difficult to have your option filled at or near the price you're looking for. Odds are the bid and offer are at some distance apart. Low volume or open interest could also spell trouble for you when you're getting out of the option as well and cut into your profits or increase your losses.

3. **Bids and Offers** Use your broker to do you some good in making trading decisions. Ask for bids and offers before you make your trading decision. Unless the market is in fast market conditions, your broker should be able to provide you a current bid and offer in just a few minutes.

4. **Brokers** Interview your broker before you make a decision on whom to trade with. Ask questions from what you've learned in this book to determine if this professional has sufficient option knowledge to assist you with your trading. You'll be surprised how many don't.

5. **Charting** Chart your options or obtain software that will chart option prices. Having accurate charts on options will help give you information on time decay, volatility movements, and changes in option demand versus the underlying futures chart. You'll have some of the most powerful information available for options.

6. **Calculator** Download or buy a good option calculator. The option forecasting techniques you've learned are excellent, but an option calculator is another tool you should add to your option arsenal.

7. **Quotes** You should find a source for reliable market quote information to keep track of your own trade positions. Unless you are an active day trader, it is probably not necessary to invest in an expensive real-time quote system or software. You can find a great deal of futures and options information for free on the Internet, usually from your broker's Web site or many of the free investment sites.

8. **Rules** Follow the basic rules we've discussed about time value, implied volatility, and buying and selling options. Set your own trading rules around the basic rules you've learned here. Evaluate your trading rules frequently and make changes when you see problems, but most important stick to them. Avoid emotional trading decisions. The once-in-a-lifetime opportunity someone might try to rush you into will likely be there tomorrow as well.

9. **Risk Management** Follow the techniques for risk management. Define your risk plan and stick to it. Some of the worst losses come from trades without a risk plan. Stick to your guns; put your risk plan on a sticky note next to the phone, or whatever you have to do to stick to your plan. You'll benefit in the long run.

10. **Monitor Trades** Keep an eye on your trades, even long-term trades. Ultimately, they are your trades no matter who recommended them to you. You should watch them carefully even if you are in a managed trading program or system. It's important for you to keep control over your positions at all times.

11. **Communication** Discuss your trading plan, risk-management plan, and trading goals with your broker or trading adviser. Make sure he or she has a good grasp on your risk tolerance and goals for making money. The more your broker knows, the better he or she can define trades that might be recommended to you

12. **Systems** Markets are often self-fulfilling prophesies. If 100,000 people are trading a particular market signal or system and 10 people are trading another, well, the first one will work, the second will not. Markets move because of the money movement of the market. Remember when considering trading systems to ask yourself why this guru is telling you what trades to make today and not doing them for himself and keeping it all a secret. First, he makes money on selling you his system. Second, if enough people do it, it will work. When they stop or move on to the next great system, it will stop.

13. **Volatility** Watch for volatility opportunities. If implied volatility reaches extremes on one side or the other, it's likely an opportunity. Make sensible trading decisions regarding volatility and define your risk, but selling high implied volatility and buying low is a key to option trading success.

14. **Profits** Let your winners ride using a risk-management strategy of trailing stops, target pricing, or option forecasting. In the end though, you won't go broke taking a profit. Take profits. Just do it!!

15. **Pay Systems** Watch out for those systems with high price tags or continuous monthly fees. These trading programs can be effective, and many are successful, but make sure you research the track record of the trader long term before investing. I've known many traders over the years paying thousands upfront or hundreds per month for systems which prove out not to work.

16. **Have Fun** Enjoy your trading whether you're doing it for a living, to build your portfolio, hedging, or just trading, it's important to keep a good attitude toward trading. Losses will happen. Keep things in perspective and move on to the next trade sticking to your plan. If you "freak out" and change everything each time you have a losing trade, you'll never identify any problem with your trading rules. Too many people jump from one method to another because of one bad trade. Research trades that don't work and evaluate if there is a problem with your analysis or if it was just an unusual market move. Change your rules if there's a real problem.

Tell your friends about this book!

FINAL EXAM

1. A derivative or futures contract is:
   (a) An employment contract for fortune tellers.
   (b) A crop insurance contract for the exchange of corn for cash.
   (c) An agreement for pink yard flamingos.
   (d) A two-party contract for the exchange of a commodity.

2. Increased crop production affects grain futures prices because
   (a) Oversupply leads to a surplus of product that may decrease price.
   (b) Traders anticipate a potential change in the balance of supply and demand and sell positions.
   (c) Foreign importers may choose to delay purchases in anticipation of lower prices.
   (d) All of the above.

3. Commodity exchanges provide which of the following?
   (a) Facilities for derivative trading
   (b) Fixed cash commodity pricing
   (c) Volatility figures for option trades

(d) None of the above

4. A call option provides:
   (a) The right to be long the underlying futures
   (b) The obligation to be long the underlying futures
   (c) Risk management on a long futures position
   (d) All of the above

5. When in the money options expire
   (a) They may be exercised into the underlying futures at the strike price.
   (b) You experience a total loss of premium.
   (c) Time value is at 0.
   (d) a and c

6. Option premium is
   (a) The quoted price of an option
   (b) The risk value of an option
   (c) a and b
   (d) None of the above

7. If the March sugar is at 850, which option is in the money?
   (a) The 750 call option.
   (b) The 875 put option
   (c) The 950 put option
   (d) All of the above

8. Which option has intrinsic value if the futures are at 8990?
   (a) The 9000 call
   (b) The 8500 put
   (c) The 8900 call
   (d) None of the above

9. If the Treasury bonds are at 110-09 the 110 call is most likely to have which delta?
   (a) 52%
   (b) 48%
   (c) 74%
   (d) 28%

10. If you purchase two January feeder cattle 100 puts with the futures at 100 your likely delta is
    (a) 50%
    (b) 100%
    (c) 200%
    (d) None of the above

11. The rate of time decay is
    (a) Alpha
    (b) Omega
    (c) Delta
    (d) Theta

12. A may corn 290 call purchased at 5 has a breakeven of
    (a) 290
    (b) 292
    (c) 295
    (d) None of the above

13. A December live cattle 82 put purchased at 0.60 and sold at 1.60 (40,000-lb contract) would have a profit of
    (a) $1000
    (b) $4000
    (c) $100
    (d) $400

14. If you were to purchase the September S&P 500 ($250 per point) 1100 put option for 15.00 and the option was exercised with futures at 1072, you would have a profit (minus trading costs) of
    (a) $4250
    (b) $3250
    (c) $7000
    (d) None of the above

15. Buying a call closer to the market and selling a call farther away is called?
    (a) Bull call spread
    (b) Long butterfly
    (c) Bear call spread

(d) Risk reversal

16. Selling a put, buying a call, and selling a call is a
    (a) Long risk reversal
    (b) Sell, buy, sell
    (c) Credit spread
    (d) None of the above

17. Buying a put at the money, selling two puts out of the money is a
    (a) Ratio put spread
    (b) Long butterfly
    (c) Butterfly
    (d) Condor

18. Buying a put at the money, selling two puts out of the money and buying one put at an even strike price difference is
    (a) Short risk reversal
    (b) Sell, buy, sell
    (c) Credit spread
    (d) Butterfly spread

19. A credit spread is
    (a) Buying put close to the money, buying farther away
    (b) Buying close to the money, selling farther away
    (c) Selling close to the money, buying farther away
    (d) None of the above

20. Buying a call and a put at the same strike price is
    (a) Double-risk reversal
    (b) Strangle
    (c) Credit spread
    (d) Straddle

21. Selling a call and selling a put at different strike prices is
    (a) Double-risk reversal
    (b) Strangle
    (c) Credit spread
    (d) Straddle

22. Selling a call close to the money and buying multiple calls out of the money is
    - (a) Short straddle
    - (b) Short risk reversal
    - (c) Long back spread
    - (d) Ratio call spread

23. Selling a put, buying a call at the same strike price would be
    - (a) Double-risk reversal
    - (b) Strangle
    - (c) Credit spread
    - (d) Synthetic futures

24. The largest risk of buying multiple out-of-the-money options is
    - (a) Time value
    - (b) What risk?
    - (c) Brokerage commissions
    - (d) Margin alls

25. Buying a March corn futures position at 220 and selling the March 240 call option for 10 would create which scenario (not including trading costs; 5000 bushes = $50/point)?
    - (a) Unlimited risk, breakeven at 210, maximum profit $1000
    - (b) Unlimited risk, breakeven at 210, maximum profit $1500
    - (c) Limited risk, breakeven at 220, maximum profit $1000
    - (d) Limited risk, breakeven at 210, maximum profit $1500

26. Option market weight describes
    - (a) Option volume or open interest at a particular strike price
    - (b) Heavy trade
    - (c) Commercials versus funds
    - (d) Increased margin

27. Hedging is described as
    - (a) Offsetting cash market risk
    - (b) Protecting input or output prices
    - (c) Improving or reducing trade risk
    - (d) All of the above

28. Hedging a cash commodity with a risk reversal is often referred to as a
    (a) Block
    (b) Synthetic future
    (c) Window
    (d) None of the above

29. Option forecasting provides you with
    (a) A guaranteed option value
    (b) A crystal ball into the future
    (c) A rough estimate based on current values
    (d) All of the above

30. The most important rule in trading futures and options is
    (a) Only risk what you can afford to lose.
    (b) Cut your losers short and let the winners ride.
    (c) Take the advice of your neighbor's cousin's friend who knows this guy who used to be a floor trader.
    (d) Pile all your money into one big trade.

ANSWERS TO EXAM

1. d. Contract for exchange of commodity.
2. d. All of the above could be a result of increased grain supply.
3. a. Exchanges provide facilities and contract specifications.
4. a. A call provides the right, but not the obligation, to be long the underlying futures contract.
5. d. Answers *a* and *c* are both correct.
6. c. Option premium is both the risk value and the quoted market price.
7. d. All of these options are in the money.
8. c. 8990 – 8900 = 90 intrinsic value.
9. a. 50% is commonly at the money, 110-09 is slightly above and would cause the 110 call to have a slightly better than 50% delta.
10. b. 100% = 2 × 50% delta.
11. d. Theta.

12. c. 295 (290 + 5).

13. d. 160 − 60 = 1.00 × \$400 or 0.01 × 40,000.

14. b. 1100 − 15 = 1085 (−1072 = 13), 13 × \$250 = \$3250.

15. a. Bull call spread.

16. b. Sell, buy, sell

17. a. Ratio put spread

18. d. Common butterfly spread.

19. c. Credit spread—selling close to money buying farther out for cover.

20. d. This is the long straddle

21. b. Short strangle

22. c. Long back spread.

23. d. Synthetic futures

24. a. Brokerage commissions are a risk, but time value decay.

25. b. 240 − 220 = 20 (+10 premium) =30, 30 × \$50 = \$1500. Naked future = unlimited risk, 220 − 10 = 210 futures breakeven.

26. a. Weight of option open interest and option volume at particular strike prices or a particular side of the market.

27. d. All are correct.

28. c. Window hedge.

29. c, Option forecasting is an estimation.

30. a. Risk only what you can afford to lose.

INDEX

A

Aggressive delta, 78–79
Ask, 20, 21
At-the-money options, 21–22
    delta of, 30
    implied volatility of, 28
    premium of, 23

B

Back spreads, 97–100
Basis, 130, 157–158
Bear put spreads, 73–74, 82, 129, 130
Bids, 20–21
    for risk reversal spread, 81
    tips for, 164
    for vertical spread, 75
"Big board," 112
Breakeven:
    exercised options, 48
    at expiration, 47–48
    prior to expiration, 46–47
    for purchased options, 46–50
    for put options, 48–51
    with risk reversal spreads, 77–78
    for short call options, 60–61
    for short put options, 61
Brokers, interviewing, 164
Bull call spreads, 70–72, 82, 129, 130
Butterfly spreads, 93–97, 116
Buy (as term), 52
Buying options, 37–50
    and breakeven, 46–50
    calls, 39–42
    puts, 42–46
    short-term, 152–153
    time value patterns in, 152

C

Cab (cabinet bid), 41
Calculators, option, 132, 136, 164
Calendar spreads, 129–131
Call back spread, 100
Call options:
    bull call spreads, 70–72
    buying, 39–42
    covered, 143–144
    defined, 18
    delta of, 30–31
    intrinsic value of, 23, 24
    ratio call spreads, 85–88
    risk reversal, 76–78
    sell, buy, sell vertical spreads, 82–83
    selling, 56–58
    short, breakeven for, 60–61
    time value of, 24
Cash replacement, 163
Cash settlement futures, 3
CBOT (Chicago Board of Trade), 5
Charting, 164
Chicago Board of Trade (CBOT), 5
Chicago Mercantile Exchange (CME), 5
Clearing firms, 6
Close, defined, 53
CME (Chicago Mercantile Exchange), 5
Combinations of futures and options, 139–142
Commercials, 4
Commodities, 1–2
    defined, 1
    hedging, 157, 158
    implied volatility of, 28
    pricing, 7–9
    specification sheets for, 17, 73
Communication with broker/advisor, 165

Condor spreads, 114–116
Contract months, 5
Covered options, 143–144
    futures covered risk reversal, 144–146
    in hedging, 160–161
Crack spreads, 163
Credit spreads, 111–114, 131

D
Day orders, 53
Day traders, 6
Defined risk, 37
Delta, 29–31
    aggressive, 78–79
    of back spreads, 97
    of bull call spreads, 72
    of butterfly spread, 98
    of calendar spreads, 130
    of long straddles, 109
    of long strangles, 103
    and margin requirements, 54
    of multiple option position, 125
    neutral, 100, 101
    of ratio spreads, 91–92
    of risk reversal, 80
    of sell, buy, sell, 84
    of straddles, 109
Derivative contracts, 2–3, 157 (*See also* Futures)

E
Electronic trading, 6
Electronic-based markets, 5, 6
E-Mini S&P 500, 5
Emotional attachment to trades/markets, 153
Exchanges, 4–6
Exercised options, breakeven for, 48
Exercising options, 17, 18, 47–48
Expiration calendar, 17
Expiration date, 17
    breakeven at, 47–48
    offsetting prior to, 62–63, 80–81
    and time decay, 25–26
    and time value, 24
    vertical spreads and selling prior to, 74–75
Expiration risk, 55

F
Fees, trading, 46
Forecasting, 135–139
Format for orders, 53
Front month, 5
Fundamental influences on market, 8–9, 153, 165
Funds, 4
Futures, 3–4
    combinations of options and, 139–142
    derivative contracts as, 2
    hedging, 157
    physical delivery vs. cash settlement, 3
    stop orders for, 154
    synthetic, 146
    trading, 5–6
Futures commission merchants, 6

G
Go long, 53
Good till cancelled (GTC), 53, 154
Greeks, 29
GTC (*see* Good till cancelled)

H
Hedgers, 3–4, 80
Hedging, 157–163
    cash replacement, 163
    commodities, 158
    covered options, 160–161
    options, 158–160
    trading vs., 158
    window hedges, 161–163

I
Implied volatility, 26–29, 131–133, 165
In-the-money options, 21–22
    delta of, 30
    exercising, 47–48
    implied volatility of, 28
Intrinsic value, 23–25, 43–44

K
Kansas City Board of Trade (KCBOT), 5

L

Legging, 85, 103
Leverage, 38
Limit orders, 63, 164
Limited gains (with short options), 54
Limited risk, 37, 48
Liquidating options, 51–52
Liquidity, 6
    and buying options, 38
    and selling options, 55
Locals, 6
Long risk reversals, 76
Long straddles, 52, 106–109
Long strangles, 100–103

M

Margin:
    for short options, 54
    when buying options, 38
Margin risk, 142
Market orders, 153–154
Market price monitoring, 154–155
Markets:
    cycles in, 64
    influences on, 8–9
    overreaction of, 89
    risk management for, 111
    as self-fulfilling prophesies, 165
    strategies for, 111
Minneapolis Grain Exchange (MGE), 5
Monetary risk points, 155–156
"The Money," 21–22
Monitoring trades, 165
Multiple option ratio spreads, 92
Multiple option strategy, 123–129
Multiple positions, 38

N

Naked short option risk, 63–64, 78
Neutral delta, 100, 101
New York Board of Trade (NYBOT), 5
New York Mercantile Exchange (NYMEX), 5
NYBOT (New York Board of Trade), 5
NYMEX (New York Mercantile Exchange), 5

O

Odds, 55
Offers, 20, 21
    for risk reversal spread, 81
    tips for, 164
    for vertical spread, 75
Offsetting, 17, 51–52
    prior to expiration, 62–63
    for risk management, 63–64
    risk reversal spreads, 80–81
    sell, buy, sell spreads, 84–85
Open, defined, 52
Open order, 53
Open outcry, 5, 20
Open stop orders, 64
Option calculators, 132, 136, 164
Option chain, 19
Option forecasting, 135–139
Option model, 41, 43–46
Options, 15–17
    combinations of futures and, 139–142
    covered, 143–146, 160–161
    defined, 15 - 16
    hedging, 158–160
    protecting, 156
    serial, 16
    short, 54
    trading, 20
Order format, 53
Out-of-the-money options, 21–22
    delta of, 30
    implied volatility of, 28
    in multiple option strategy, 123–124
    premium of, 23

P

Pay systems, 166
Physical delivery of commodities, 3
Pits, 5
P&L (*see* Profit and loss)
Potential, 38
Premium, 19–21
    for calls, 40–41
    and implied volatility, 27
    inflated, entering market with, 89–90

Premium (*Cont.*):
    for puts, 42–45
    repurchase, 64
    stops based on, 64
    theta and potential loss of, 26
Premium levels strategy, 155
Price:
    ask, 20, 21
    delta and change in, 29–31
    market price monitoring strategy,
        154–155
    option premium, 19–21
    strike, 16, 21
    and supply and demand, 7–9
    and "the money," 21–22
    of underlying futures, 40–44
Pricing:
    of commodities, 7–9
    of futures contracts, 3
Profit and loss (P&L), 58, 60, 156
    with bear put spreads, 73–74
    with bull call spreads, 70–71
Profit taking, 156–157, 165
Put back spread, 100
Put options, 18–19
    bear put spreads, 73–74
    breakeven for, 48–51
    covered, 143–144
    defined, 18
    delta of, 31
    intrinsic value of, 23, 25
    ratio put spreads, 90–91
    risk reversal, 79–80
    sell, buy, sell vertical spreads, 84
    selling, 59–60
    short, breakeven for, 61
    time value of, 25

Q
Quote page, 19, 20, 136–137
Quotes, sources for, 164

R
Rate of time decay, 26
Ratio spreads, 85–92
    advantage of, 88–89

Ratio spreads (*Cont.*):
    calendars in, 131
    call, 85–88
    delta of, 91–92
    multiple option, 92
    put, 90–91
Repurchase, low premium, 64
Resistance levels, 80, 158
Risk:
    with back spreads, 99
    with bull call spreads, 72
    with butterfly spread, 95–96
    with calendar spreads, 130–131
    defined, 37
    expiration, 55
    with long straddles, 108
    margin, 142
    with naked short options, 63–64
    with selling call options, 57–58
    with selling put options, 60
    with short options, 54, 55
    with short strangles, 105
    with stop orders, 140
    when buying options, 37, 48
Risk management, 151–163
    hedging for, 157–163
    offsetting for, 63–64
    by removing trades prior to expiration,
        75
    stop orders for, 140
    strategies for, 153–157
    time value management for, 151–153
    tips for, 165
Risk profile, 139, 140
Risk reversal put options, 79–80
Risk reversal spreads, 76–81
    advantage of, 80
    aggressive delta with, 78–79
    long, 76
    offsetting prior to expiration, 80–81
    risk reversal put options, 79–80
    short, 76
Risk value, 23 (*See also* Time value)
Round turn, 46
Rules, trading, 165

S

Sell, buy, sell vertical spreads, 82–85
Selling options, 53–61
  advantages of, 55–56
  and breakeven, 60–61
  calls, 56–58
  defined, 52
  disadvantages of, 54–55
  puts, 59–60
  time value patterns in, 152
Serial options, 16
Short options, 54
  breakeven for, 60–61
  call, 60–61
  put, 61
  stop orders for, 154
  (*See also* Selling options)
Short risk reversals, 76
Short sell, buy, sell, 84
Short straddles, 109–111
Short strangles, 104–106
Short-term purchasing, 152–153
Slippage, 140
Specification sheets, 17, 73
Speculators, 4, 80
Spreads:
  back, 97–100
  butterfly, 93–97
  calendar, 129–131
  condor, 114–116
  crack, 163
  credit, 111–114
  long straddles, 106–109
  long strangles, 100–103
  risk reversal, 76–81
  short straddles, 109–111
  short strangles, 104–106
  vertical, 69–75, 82–85
Stop orders, 63, 140
  based on premium, 64, 155
  monetary, 155–156
  for risk management, 153–154
  trailing, 156
Strike price, 16, 21
  and implied volatility, 27

Strike price (*Cont.*):
  put vs. call, 31
  defined, 16
Supply and demand, 7–9
Support levels, 80, 158
Synthetic futures, 146
Systems:
  pay, 166
  trading, 165

T

Taking profits, 156–157, 165
Technical chart management, 63
Technical influences on markets, 9, 153
Theta, 26
Time decay, 25–26
  with bull call spreads, 72
  and buying options, 38
  forecasting with, 137–139
  with long straddles, 103, 108
  managing, 151–153
  with multiple option strategy,
    126–127
  with ratio spreads, 91
  and selling options, 55
  with short strangles, 105
Time value, 23–25
  of calls, 40–41
  management of, 151–153
  of puts, 43
  researching, 152
To close, defined, 53
To open:
  defined, 52
  spread order technique for, 75
Trades, monitoring, 165
Trading:
  analyzing trading decisions, 125
  and breakeven, 46–50, 60–61
  buying calls, 39–42
  buying puts, 42–46
  fees for, 46
  futures, 5–6
  hedging vs., 158
  options, 20

Trading (*Cont.*):
    rules for, 165
    selling calls, 56–58
    selling puts, 59–60
    (*See also specific strategies*)
Trading floor, 5
Trading systems, 165
Trailing stops, 156
Treasury futures, 106

U
Unlimited potential, 38
Unlimited risk (with short options), 54

V
Value:
    forecasting, 137–139
    futures fluctuation in, 21
    intrinsic, 23–25, 43–44
    option premium, 19–21
    risk, 23
    time, 23–25

Vertical spreads, 69–75
    bear put spreads, 73–74
    bull call spreads, 70–72
    defined, 69
    sell, buy, sell, 82–85
    selling prior to expiration, 74–75
VOI (volume and open interest), 164
Volatility:
    and buying options, 38
    with calendar spreads, 130
    with credit spreads, 111
    implied, 26–29, 131–133, 165
    as opportunity, 165
    with ratio spreads, 88
    seasonal, 128
    and selling options, 55
Volatility analysis—market weight strategy, 131–135
Volume and open interest (VOI), 164

W
Window hedges, 161–163
"Windows," 80

ABOUT THE AUTHOR

Kevin M. Kraus is currently the president of CSM Futures Group a Texas based retail futures and options brokerage firm. He is also author and editor of *CSM Futures Trade Outlook* and *Market News*. Kevin has also written daily option market commentary and analysis for DTN, Futuresource and FarmDayta market information providers, as well as appearing weekly on radio business talk shows. Kevin coauthored two top-selling option instructional videos and is creator of Kevin Kraus's Option Tutor Course and Option Basics option education courses. For more information, visit his Web site at www.kkraus.com.